As a memoir, *Turn to Me* is written with McNamara's candor and emotional honesty. It provides real life assurances that inner peace of heart and mind are attainable for everyone here, now, and beyond. *Turn to Me* gently encourages each to seek their own paths of healing and to realize its spiritual guidance, as I have. With depth of meaning and solace during these dark times, *Turn to Me* is a gift waiting to be read.

—Sue Whan, Editor

A gifted healer reflects on her own inward journey as she reads the personal revealing notes her mother left behind. The contrast and similarities of their lives create an insightful and inspiring message.

—Jeanne Crane, Author of Amidst the Stones

A touching and insightful biography of a multi-generational quest for peace. Janice offers us a first-person view of her search for answers to life struggles while skillfully incorporating diary entries from her mother's personal testimony of how and where she found her own solutions to challenges faced. As readers, we are shown how blind faith and surrender can create miraculous solutions that, for this family, became mere normal occurrences in their everyday life. Along this journey, we discover how Janice was able to turn her feelings of anger and resentment from her tumultuous mother/daughter relationship into one of mutual love and deep respect. Thank you, Janice, for this work and allowing me the opportunity to reflect on my relationship with both my own mother and the divine creator!!

—Jason A, IT Entrepreneur, medium and seeker

"Healing often occurs simply through having the opportunity to express misdirected thoughts, seeing the truth of any situation, and making room for miracles."(Janice McNamara, RN)

First in her role as teacher of *A Course in Miracles*, and later as my Reiki Master, God has been using Janice as guide for me to see my own light as a long-time trauma survivor. She provides a safe space to have such opportunities to see the truth in any situation and encourages me to make room for miracles. Whatever way manifests for me, may my own healing lead to the place of peace within myself that Janice represents and shows to those who are fortunate enough to cross her path.

—Maggie Maloy, student of *A Course in Miracles*, Fairport, NY

"In no order of hierarchy, Loved Ones, Ascended Masters, Spirit or Animal Guides patiently shepherd each of us on our own way until eventually, we trust our inner wise counsel."

Such is the essence of Janice McNamara's book, *Turn to Me*. As a teacher of *A Course in Miracles* and as a minister, her accounting struck many chords because I am a true believer of receiving messages from beyond the thin veil.

Turn to Me is an intriguing narration of Janice's personal spiritual development while she navigates her transcendent, evolving path. I was drawn in by the author's accidental uncovering of her mother's notes, which helped define the matriarch's faith experiences. This is a page-turner that I didn't want to put down as I discovered the many encounters Janice personally experienced with the spirit world.

—Rev. Barb Adams, Author of *The Adventures of the Course Kids: Through Faith and Grace*

This is a beautifully written book for those on a path of spiritual exploration and healing. Janice McNamara shares personal, multi-generational stories to reveal lessons and insights that I found to be very relatable. Her personal journey provides guidance, encouraging my own self-exploration.

This is an inspirational and thought-provoking book. Thank you, Janice, for sharing your story and your wisdom.

—Pat Wall

Turn to Me is a captivating story of parallel spiritual journeys of healing and forgiveness. After finding a collection of notes written by her mother, McNamara realizes that, like herself, her mother experienced a spiritual awakening and even, that her mother channeled Jesus. Through reading and recording her mother's notes, McNamara gains a new understanding of her mother and comes to know her in an unexpected new way: spiritually! *Turn to Me* traces not only McNamara's discoveries about her mother, but also her own spiritual journey—her gradual awareness of the importance of soul-searching and turning within, in meditative stillness, to discover her authentic self. Her book fills the reader with hope, as she shows that spiritual awakening is possible for all of us. McNamara also explores the fascinating idea that healing can occur beyond the grave. *Turn to Me* is a reminder that it is never too late to find forgiveness and healing, even after a person has passed.

—Heather Hutton, M.A., Instructor of English

McNamara takes the reader on a journey from her mother's exploration of God and Jesus, and her attempts to incorporate spirituality into her own life as a wife and mother, to McNamara's own spiritual development and discovery of the metaphysical. McNamara's spiritual growth followed directly in the wake of her mother's experiences, leading eventually to a career in holistic medicine, her development as an intuitive and ultimately in her understanding of the oneness and inter-connectedness of all. Her experiences as an intuitive reminds us that life does not end with the death of the physical body, but that learning and loving continues across the veil. For those of us on a spiritual journey of our own, both McNamara's life lessons and her mother's channeling experiences provide valuable lessons to help us along the way.

—Glenda Brayman

JANICE McNAMARA, RN

Turn
To
Me

My Mother's Notebooks, My Journey,
and A Gift of Forgiveness

First printing 2024

Published by Next Step Holistic Publishing

Printed in the United States of America.

Cover design: Amy Miller

Editing and internal formatting: Francisca de Zwager

For information: 625 Panorama Trail, Building 2, Suite 190, Rochester, NY. 14625 and www.nextstepholistic.com

ISBN: 979-8-218-40888-6
Library of Congress Control Number: 2024908218

In honor of my mother, Frances

In loving memory of all those who have passed on
and reached out beyond the veil to bring us the
wisdom of their journey

Invitation

Many loved ones leave behind powerful treasures that appear in their own time, bringing meaning, direction, and purpose. The treasure that found its way into my heart was from my mother's cluttered television stand drawers. Varied sized notebooks filled with pages of her familiar handwriting drew my attention to the many things I did not understand about my mother.

Gathering at our local Catholic church on the eastern coastline of Massachusetts where I grew up, my mother met with a few friends to form a charismatic group in the early 1980s. Although the church no longer supported her group, they continued to meet in the church. Here, she could channel messages from Jesus to the group and record His teachings in these mysterious notebooks I now held in my hands. My Aunt Kay, my mother's older sister, was among those who met to share His teachings.

Pursuing the meaning of these personal and group messages from Jesus eventually led mom to see her life from a new perspective. Simultaneously,

I was exploring the mysteries of my life in a very different way. My mother and I did not see eye to eye on most matters, and neither of us understood the other or was aware that separate but parallel paths existed under the surface of our roles as mother and daughter.

Having a separate experience with Jesus, I would soon realize that for both my mother and me, Jesus always came to us as a non-denominational Ascended Master, wanting only for us to remember the truth of our divinity. Even though my path differed from my mother's, His mission in working with us was the same—to help lift the veils of our past experiences to find joy and inner peace in the present.

Ascended Masters, such as Jesus, are ones who came to full enlightenment while walking this earth. I have learned to be sensitive to the Ascended Masters among us, as they come now with a very important agenda if we are open to receive their gentle, divine help. They present themselves to each of us in a way we readily understand through vision, hearing and/or as a special feeling or intuition. This is not a religious experience, but one of healing our limited thoughts at the deepest level and one of trusting that, with knowledge of this guidance, we are never alone. They come and go supporting us depending on where we are on our spiritual path. Most importantly, they always appear gently as a trusted friend whom you would eagerly welcome.

It took a great deal of time for my mother and me to grow spiritually. I wrote *Turn to Me* to inspire others to look within as we did, see the healing potential in all relationships, and discover the steps to arrive at a place of self-love and self-forgiveness. By sharing my story and hers, my prayer for you is to find a sense of inner peace by reaching beyond the constraints of the mind and trusting your own unlimited experience.

My mother's treasure of notebooks is a gift and an example of guidance for all of us. Her process of self-exploration was not common for suburban housewives in her time. It took courage to pursue a deeper meaning of life by connecting to a path and a group that supported her. I unknowingly watched from a distance, curious, without fully grasping how she was exploring ways to improve her life. I knew she was beginning to be more kind and drawn to the yearnings of her heart rather than being led only through the responsibilities assigned to her as a wife and mother.

Turn to Me will lead you on a journey of letting go of the past, bringing you from fear, anger, and frustration to a place of love and self-acceptance, and help you find your true essence. You will discover the value of family experience and how difficult relationships are simply a call to your own healing. I invite you to join me as we turn to Jesus, our ancestors, and each other for much needed guidance. Let us embrace the seeds my mother planted so beautifully.

For enhanced clarity, I have divided the book into three sections. Part I consists of My Mother's Notebooks, Part 2 delves into My Journey, and Part 3 explores A Gift of Forgiveness.

Janice McNamara

Part I

My Mother's Notebooks

Chapter One

I stared at the brown wooden stairs leading to the front enclosed porch of my family home on a busy secondary street. As I neared the entrance, thoughts of sleeping on the porch during hot summer nights flooded my mind. It was a modest three bedroom, two floor, single home with a large backyard that embraced the commotion of six children and many celebrations.

One minute I was having a familiar and predictable existence. Next, I was nearing a moment for which I felt unprepared. Heaviness filled my heart with the life-changing news I was about to deliver to my mother. My mind was racing as I recalled what I loved about my life here—the sense of belonging to my family, shared moments with longtime friends, and a newly opened office. I began to climb the stairs, carefully contemplating each familiar step.

That day was the beginning of November 1999. My husband, Jack, had taken a job in Upstate, New York, which meant I would leave these familiar and comfortable surroundings of the Northeast—those I had not strayed far from growing up.

As I entered the kitchen, walking straight back from the front door through a small hallway, I found my mother at the table, grateful for the visit. I was not ready to sit down quite yet, so I poured myself a warm cup of coffee, holding the mug, and leaning against the counter as if it would offer me the courage to share my news with her. How was I going to say this? I barely understood what it entailed to leave my home. Although there was a past strained relationship with my mother, we had reached one of mutual respect, but now would I be disappointing her again? My inner struggle continued as my thoughts moved to her recent diagnosis of Alzheimer's.

Within my protective wall constructed to hold back the anticipated emotional tide, I managed to find the right moment to announce the painful news. Once spoken, my mother made an equally awkward attempt to hide how my moving would affect her. I welcomed her need for details of the move to overshadow the distress I was feeling about changing my life so abruptly. Moving would also be difficult, as our relationship was on the mend; not to mention how I was to care for her from such a distance.

After my husband and I settled into our new home in a suburb of Rochester, NY, my mother began a further descent into a world of confusion. Quickly, she went from partial care at home to an assisted living facility. I drove back monthly to see her and help my siblings manage her care the best I could.

During the necessary drives back and forth from my new home, I noticed I was slowly detaching from my life in Massachusetts.

Finally, we decided to sell the family home. My son Jason, my four sisters—Ann, Alice, Mary, Carol—and my brother, Bill, with their spouses gathered over several days to clear forty years of accumulation, while desperately holding onto the memories.

During this process, I found myself assigned to the small living room that once accommodated eight people. I imagined the many holiday dinners spilling out from the dining area to the adjacent living room.

As my attention wandered back to the room, I found myself spending far too much time traveling on memory lane and less time packing. My siblings and I couldn't help but yell back and forth to each other over each long-forgotten treasure we discovered.

Starting with the television stand, I began gathering notebooks and papers that I knew were written during my mother's time in the charismatic group in the 1980s. After a fleeting moment of feeling like an intruder upon her privacy, I carefully opened the notebooks that I held with curiosity in my hands. Never having been interested in reading them in the past, I was surprised to feel elated at the prospect of delving into them later. I packed them away for a time when I could give them more attention.

The time to revisit the notebooks finally came in December 2015 when I was intuitively led back to explore this one thing left of my mother's belongings that would bring me closer to knowing her. Home with an awful cold and a broken washing machine, I could not travel back east for the holidays. The opportunity arose to do the unthinkable–relax! When I felt better and realized I had the gift of a full week off, I pulled out my laptop. Little did I know what was in store for me!

Soon after reading and catching up on emails, an overwhelming need to gather my mother's notebooks from my files took hold. I could not explain it at the time, but I felt guided by a mysterious force to set my laptop aside and jump up from the sofa. Eagerly, I climbed the stairs to find the notebooks in a drawer right where I had left them years earlier.

Reading page after page of faded ink and penciled entries, it became clear to me these beautiful messages needed to be preserved. My mother had apparently recorded the teachings of Jesus as He spoke through her to the group. It was as if a beacon of light shone through these notes, guiding me towards something very familiar. Each entry made such exquisite sense to me and validated my then understanding of how letting go of people and things I no longer had control over was the only way back to that one purpose of knowing myself.

One entry that struck me was Jesus telling the group that they must perform their own work, each must be a friend to one another, but no one can do the work assigned to another and manage to do the work assigned to themselves if the work is to be well done in His name.

I had not understood it in the 1980s when the group formed; however, when I read her notes later, I came to see how my mother had moved from a place of worry and fear about me and my siblings to a more peaceful space of letting go and allowing for the guidance of Jesus.

The more entries I read, the clearer it was that I needed to share them with my family, as they were as much in the dark as I was about the group. We had all always been curious about what happened at the church and in those meetings.

After reading the notebooks, I undertook to transcribe her notes on my laptop. While I was typing, the teacher in me was compelled to explain the passages. These explanations began forming chapters. Before I knew it, this was a much bigger project than I expected and a mission that took me far beyond the preservation of these notebooks and into a new perception of my own life puzzle.

The overall sense I had from the messages in the notebooks was that Jesus was supporting the group members—my mother, my Aunt Kay, and their friends. He was helping them with their life experiences, guiding them to look within, and teaching them how to take care of themselves in difficult times. He taught them to let go of the need to fix others' problems and to focus on putting themselves first, resting in prayer with Him, and turning seemingly insurmountable problems over to Him.

Jesus spoke to the group each time they met from April 1982 to December 1984. This book is created on the foundation of His teachings passed on in this charismatic group and my own experience of self-exploration.

According to my brother Bill, a deacon in the Catholic Church, "The form of prayer that Spirit is directing to them seems to be meditative and quiet. The writing and tone of Jesus is so different from hers. I don't think Mom's or her friends' words would be phrased like those which were written down. They must have been inspired. I thought those words given to them were through prophetic gifts, in English, though. I see these words were passed on in Tongues and the notebooks reflected the English translation."

My mother allowed this beautiful gift of speaking and interpreting the language of Tongues to flow through her. Because of her need for privacy, it is not clear when she began to speak in this way or if this was how she received Jesus in every group. One day in the early 1980s I remember her speaking in Tongues at our house with my Aunt Kay. Carefully entering the room to hear more clearly, I felt I was intruding as I immersed myself in the sounds of a verbal expression of something that demanded respect but was unlike prayer or chanting. When they noticed me, they abruptly stopped and made light of my observation. Our family, including me, did not understand what occurred in the charismatic group at the time. Unfortunately, we called Mom "St. Frances" in a teasing way to hide our discomfort of something so mysterious. Later, I would learn this was not as secretive as it appeared.

Although my mother received messages from Jesus through gatherings in the charismatic group, He can appear to anyone at any time or any place. He was and still is available to everyone as an Ascended Master, a spiritually enlightened being, bringing healing, love, and non-judgmental guidance. Having worked with Jesus myself through meditation or during a walk, I bring His words to you because I experience the same support, understanding, and peace my mother enjoyed. I noticed His guidance comes more clearly when I give up the need to know why or how He will convey His divine messages to me.

Recalling the time when I realized the teachings of Jesus from my mother's group could become a story, I initially felt fear and doubt. My apprehension in taking on such an endeavor got in the way of my accepting what I was meant to do. My prior writing experience had been limited to one creative writing workshop, Stephen King's book "*On Writing*," notes or letters to family and friends, and weekly scientific nursing papers. All those avenues were helpful; however, the flow of writing only came with the effortless connection to divine guidance. Jesus's words became clearer the more I listened to my heart. Simple acknowledgment of my doubts and fears made room for the words. The true perception of my story and my mother's eventually found its way to the pages, making itself known for me to share with my readers.

Chapter Two

Not until I was in my thirties did I understand that the conflicts between my mother and me may have been fueled not only by a rebellious teen but also by her own childhood experience. My Aunt Florence, my mother's oldest sister, revealed to me some of those difficulties they both had growing up– ones my mother had not been willing to express. Since my earliest memories, Mom's responses to me always seemed tinged with anger and frustration. These interactions with her intensified during my teens as I struggled to gain independence. Every disagreement I had with her pushed me further and further away.

Despite my inability to understand the source of our conflict, the stage was set to view my mother differently. I explored avenues that would eventually bring us to a better place in our relationship.

My journey started with, and was affected by, reading self-help books like Nancy Friday's *My*

Mother, Myself and Norman Vincent Peale's *The Power of Positive Thinking.* I later joined support groups and learned meditation and yoga practices.

In 1998, I set up a private practice after studying the subtle energy modalities of Reiki and Polarity, and, after moving to New York State, Advanced Holistic Wellness and Spiritual Psychology. This training, coupled with my intuition, allows me to work with clients to help them uncover underlying thoughts and beliefs, to reconnect with their authentic selves, and empower them to nurture their intuition, expand awareness, and infuse joy into every aspect of life.

Around 2013, I was introduced to the channeled teachings of Jesus from The Foundation of Inner Peace, *A Course in Miracles.* These messages and teachings made me fully aware that there is nothing outside of us that isn't about our healing and remembering the light of who we are.

I found all of these resources to be ways of removing obstacles I believed stood in the way of my physical well-being and spiritual evolution. They opened the way to understanding my mother's earlier life experiences and how she gradually changed while on her own private quest for peace through the charismatic group.

In my late twenties, I delighted in seeing my mother, who was attending these meetings, shift from an antagonistic demeanor to a calm one, even if it was a change I couldn't understand. What I did know was that our relationship slowly improved and my acceptance of her grew.

With this new ease between my mother and me, I trusted her enough to attend one of her meetings. I was struggling with a concussion when she encouraged me to attend a group healing session that was open to the public. She told me the meeting was in the main part of the church and there were group members and others who would be there. Desperate to feel better, I accepted that prayer and laying on of hands was a part of the practice. Little did I know that years later I would follow in my mother's footsteps when I explored the hands on healing of Reiki.

At one point, a group member came to me and placed her hand on my head while I was standing. She said a prayer, then guided me to my seat with the gentle pressure of her hand. I didn't know what to make of it. The symptoms of my injury eased.

What I couldn't explain was tucked away in my mind.

Each day, as I continued to transcribe the teachings onto my laptop, I was guided to include certain entries that turned out to be the most important and relevant messages to the benefit of many of us today. One significant lesson translated from my mother's notebooks is to turn our worries and concerns over to Jesus. There were times I perceived my mother did this at the expense of working out solutions and communicating better with me. It disturbed me, but I imagine the walls I had built around me contributed to her frustration.

My mother became highly conscious that her old way of responding with anger in the family was not working. Letting go of her need to fix everything and turning our lives and her own over to Jesus in prayer afforded her a more peaceful alternative, allowing each of us to grow in our own way and at our own pace.

My sister Alice shared that my mother was always enthusiastic about going to the group meetings and she would occasionally hear her talking about it with my Aunt Kay in the kitchen, where all conversations usually ceased when one of us entered.

Mom prayed not only in the group, but at home for all of us. When Alice went into labor with her first child, the baby was in breech position. Soon after my mother sent prayers to her, the baby, unassisted, shifted in the womb for a normal delivery—a gift of physical healing. Somehow my mother knew that before Alice knew. How many experiences have we all had of *just knowing* that we chose to ignore? I believe my mother was very conscious of these "knowing" situations and considered them a normal part of her life.

One afternoon years later, sitting down over a rare lunch out with my mother, I bravely asked her if she would say something in Tongues. Knowing our relationship had reached a point of respect and one she trusted, without hesitation, she began speaking in this beautiful sacred language. When she stopped, she used the paper dinner napkin to record the interpretation. She was clearly capable of both speaking and interpreting. I regret not saving that napkin, but I do remember the tone and words she wrote were like the reflective guided messages in the notebooks.

The writings from the charismatic group occurred before the Harmonic Convergence, which occurred in August 1987. That convergence only happens every ten thousand years. This is a time when planets align and spiritual energy is greatly amplified, causing our levels of consciousness to increase on Earth. Unaware of this significant event then, it was the time my spiritual journey began.

In the ongoing process of having this wonderful energy to support our awakening, it also brings up into our awareness latent feelings, thoughts, beliefs, and memories. When that happens, we are not to fear them but simply to acknowledge and honor what no longer serves our purpose, then let them pass through. At times, it may seem like things are falling apart—jobs, relationships, and health—however, our awareness builds from each experience during these times, and when things settle, we can see those disruptive moments as a gift of renewed stability.

Jesus refers to changing times and darker times ahead in one of the group's entries. In the notebook writings, He was preparing the group to take care of themselves during these times and to rest, to be present to hear His word, and to pray and be guided by Him. One of His powerful messages is to focus on self-healing rather than to invest personal energy on chaos around us when such events occur. The group's mission was to heal and comfort their families and the community—a mission I seem to have been subtly prepped for.

Much later, the self-discovery I was exploring helped to lift the veils as I slowly began to awaken and become more keenly mindful of my judgments, actions, and thoughts. Even though I had become calmer and more centered, more like my mother, I often felt as if I were taking an uncommon, less traveled path. Then, as the desire to connect with others took hold, the right people began to appear one by one on this journey of awakening. They surrounded me with their knowledge, wisdom, and experience, which helped me to understand why my mother valued the healing companionship found in group settings.

Chapter Three

Introduction to the Teachings

Staring at the small stack of three spiral notebooks of varying sizes, I was unaware of the mysteries that would unfold within their pages. My first thought was that of grade school. It was as if my mother had pulled the lined notebooks from the leftover stock of school supplies in the house, without a care, to fulfill one purpose—getting every word from Jesus carefully recorded.

Glancing over the worn entries in pencil and ink, I felt the comfort of her presence. Emerging from the pages was her familiar longhand way of writing, slanted to the right and somewhat like mine. It held so many memories of seeing her signature on school papers, absent notes, letters, and birthday cards. Not knowing shorthand, she must have had to record quickly. After I had spent many hours deciphering the notebooks in the beginning, finding single letters in some sentences, it was a relief to find her personal shorthand code in one of the books. Each treasured entry in the group of notebooks left the reader with a signature statement from this gentle being representing himself as "Jesus."

Included with the journals was a book by Don Basham called *"A Handbook on Tongues Interpretation and Prophecy,"* a small soft covered book describing the saints, along with retreat flyers and newspaper clippings of charismatic conferences. Further exploration revealed a tiny spiral notebook containing my mother's method of prayer for individual family members. It showed me how actively she was releasing worries and showed me how she set aside her own agenda for me, trusting Him and His plan.

An example of this prayer mentioned later during a speech she gave, is *"Oh Heavenly Father, in the name of Your Son, Jesus, I lift to you Janice, this day. Lead her, guide her, show her the way to your Heavenly Kingdom. Let this be Your will."*

The focus Jesus had for my mother was to guide her towards self-discovery despite her perpetual need to help others. Although the prayers were an important part of her journey, she tended to get involved emotionally with the problems of others at the expense of her own healing. One message was, *Keep pressing on to hear My word.* I believe this next response summarizes His multiple replies to my mother when she raised concern for another person. *Seek not the reasons. Concentrate on the solutions. I am the way, the truth, and the light. Only through me will they find the peace they are seeking. My arms are opened to them, but they do not come to me. The bitterness is not from Me. I will give them peace. I stand and I wait for them. They must return to me.*

Jesus emphasizes all we need to do to find inner peace is to be present and willing to turn over our distress to Him. He wants us to "press on." My mother's prayers held great value when she could hand over worries to Him and detach from the need for an outcome. As He says, *Pray for each. The prayers and thanksgiving of thousands will reach my heavenly Father.* Looking back, I believe I have been the recipient of her prayers many times.

Entries in the notebooks were messages specific to each group member and others more general to the whole group. However, what captivated me the most was how similar the short and direct statements were to messages I have heard from Jesus. Words such as *"See through my eyes"* were crucial when I needed to see things from a place of non-judgment. At other times, He would convey loving, healing messages to my clients during their sessions if they were open to a connection. Also, Jesus occasionally appeared while I journaled or meditated as a reminder that He is always with me. Most of the time, He begins with, *"Dear one, I am here,"* as he patiently waits for me to turn to Him. The experience of His presence helped me to realize why my mother was so dedicated to following His guidance.

After sorting through the notebooks and papers my mother entrusted to their prospective steward, I used every free moment I had under the cover of the winter months to preserve each precious word. My eager intent was to share them with the family. It was a pleasure to enter each soothing and comforting message from Jesus into the computer, which would quickly and beautifully improve my dismal thinking.

Since the beginning of this endeavor, I have held an image of my mother entering the church to attend the group, with her back to a world she temporarily leaves behind. I see her wearing her powder blue cardigan sweater and knee length gray skirt. Knowing that many times the heat would be turned down in the church meeting room during off hours in the winter months, I envision her pulling on an extra layer more tightly around her, internalizing her discomfort to keep herself warm. I also see her sitting quietly, absorbing the guiding, supportive, and uplifting words of Jesus as she quickly wrote down every word He said. Her determination became clear when she consistently dedicated time each week to meet with others who shared her quest. I cherished my time reading and rereading all one hundred twenty notebook entries that were recorded between April 20, 1982 and December 27, 1984. Amazed at the revelations, they significantly changed my perception of my mother.

I considered the length and the personal messages to the group and decided to include only those messages most relatable and most in alignment with the struggles we all face today. Jesus prepared the group for challenging times by helping to build their trust and to show them how to release their worries related to work, relationships, family, and health.

From my first impulse to gather the notebooks to the development of the contents, I was not writing this book alone. As I reinforced each of the messages from Jesus, a new truth and awareness was revealed: the knowledge that support, guidance, and love are attainable. To integrate the teachings at a deeper level, I found it necessary to pause often, especially when the words resonated in my heart. If the words stopped flowing or I was not feeling the desire to write, I would accept the need to step back and stay open to the next guided step. The purpose of writing this book evolved from my intention to preserve the notebooks for my family to sharing an unexpected story of forgiveness—with readers, seekers, and those beyond my known circle.

The teachings of Jesus from my mother's notebooks took her on a restorative journey, changing her many adverse reactions to the life she had chosen. Noticing the similarities, I was not far behind her in my quest for the same understanding. We both were led to discover our purpose through group gatherings and channelled messages, and we were able to bring the wisdom of that experience to the community.

The following writings are word for word as best I can read Mom's handwriting. I have not included all entries because of their length or the need for privacy of individual group members. Occasionally, I had to add a word or two she may have missed. It seemed Mom was taking rapid dictation without the skill of shorthand.

I invite you to experience this journey with me and enjoy your own personal interpretations of the teachings of Jesus.

I do not come to speak of things that you do not know.

I come not to use words which do not already abide within you.

I do not come with the wisdom that you do not already contain.

I do not come with a love grander than that which already flowers within the silent places of your own Heart.

I do not come to place Himself above you. I come only to walk as an equal beside you.

—Jesus

The Way of Mastery by The Shanti Christo Foundation

Chapter Four

"Sit with me in silence, my love, that I can commune with you in the depths of your heart, for that is where I love to speak to you best of all." —Jesus

It is difficult to reach the place Jesus asks us to go. The moment our eyes close, our attention turns to many random thoughts in the mind and feelings in our bodies. This noise in the mind prevents clear communication with Him and keeps us far from the heart where all the knowing exists.

Prior to learning meditation, one experience that started my search for meaning in my life began in the mid-1970s as a twenty-two-year-old. I attended an Al-Anon meeting to support a friend. With alcohol abuse-related problems in her family, it was a beneficial organization to help sort out the impact alcoholism had on her. The meeting was my first opportunity to sit still in this type of setting where each person was allowed to speak without the interruptions I was used to at home. Being present to Dawna and the various speakers, I could soon feel the effect of their words. I felt right at home! Was there alcohol in my family? Did I have too many drinks on the weekends? I couldn't count the number of times I turned in astonishment to my older sister, Ann, who had also come along. The speaker's stories were all too familiar.

Confused at first, I knew my parents did not drink or keep alcohol in the house while we were children. Yet I was hearing many similar signs and behaviors, as if I had an encounter with an alcoholic at home. I would later question my maternal grandfather's use of alcohol. The emotions of anger, frustration, and fear my mother displayed at home certainly fit the picture.

With the help of this experience, my awareness of my own behaviors and the effect they had on decisions, relationships, and health kept me on a journey to search for answers that would help me make sense of my life and feel more settled.

The next prompt that led me to consider the value of silence and change my intended career direction occurred following a car accident in 1984 while I was in college. This accident resulted in a chronic foot injury that altered how I now practice nursing. During recovery and rehabilitation, I was exposed to a world of alternative methods for calming and pain control. One such method was acupuncture. Noticing the difficulty I had fully relaxing on her table, this practitioner was brave enough to suggest I practice meditation. The suggested five minutes seemed a reasonable challenge, so that day, I went home and sat on the living room sofa. As soon as I closed my eyes, the random thoughts of the day flooded in, making it difficult to be still. After many attempts to quiet intrusive, repetitive thoughts, I could finally set them aside.

Working with patients in a hospital setting offered another opportunity to practice being in the moment with each person to fully assess their needs and help them lower their stress level.

One day in the clinic, I helped a physician with a delicate and serious procedure on an anxious patient. Despite words of encouragement, the closer we came to starting, the patient began screaming and curled her arms up over her face. She was not in physical pain; however, I suspected her reaction was heightened by the shadows of many past, invasive procedures. While the doctor gave me space to work with her, he cautiously stepped back from the sterile field, and I asked her to focus on me. When she finally dropped her hands from her face and took some deep breaths with me, she let go of her fear, becoming calmer and more centered. We were all relieved, and the procedure went quickly and more comfortably than she had anticipated.

The years to follow were filled with events that gave me the opportunity to practice being present to all thoughts and feelings. Five minutes turned into one to two hours or more of stillness in my mind. There are always times when it is difficult to stay focused; however, when I wander too far from the stillness, I only craved it more. My ability to relax improved dramatically.

Again, this spiritual journey on earth is not without both personal and global distractions. How we interpret and deal with them depends on our state of mind. Continually looking at my emotions, beliefs, and blocks to moving forward, I have discovered through my practice that the interferences become less and less. Then, being present to His guidance becomes clearer.

I can imagine my mother knew this pathway of healing well through prayer or rosary. The stillness Jesus speaks of is not easily attained without dedication to the practice of being present with ourselves. The rosary was one physical way for my mother to shift out of fearful negative thoughts into a place of allowing His guidance to come to her. She would achieve serenity, repeating the Lord's Prayer or Hail Mary's, while holding each bead. These prayers, like mantras, became the way she used to turn her attention inward to find her own stillness.

DECEMBER 20, 1982

"Listen to my word, only my word, and I will guide the ministries to carry on my work. They must listen to me and let me guide them. I need the cooperation of all leaders." — Jesus

On this day, Jesus emphasized the need for the group to awaken to His guidance. I can sense the urgency in this message as He expresses the need to pass down his teachings to those who are ready to receive them. My mother was yearning for a change in her life, and I can imagine this invitation from Him was the focus she needed. It is amazing, and a wonderful discovery, how my mother heard His messages so clearly, could record them word for word, then incorporate them into her life.

My encounters with Jesus were different in some ways. For me, He would come when I was in a less formal setting, teaching or guiding me to teach others. During my time with him, I realized it was important to heal my mind before I could fully embrace His guidance and wisdom. Only then could I show the light of that awareness to others.

The first obstacle I faced in sharing my light involved sharing my personal journey with a client. In nursing, we were taught not to share such experiences. This always confused me, making me feel as though I was withholding a part of myself and my journey that may be helpful. Eventually, by trusting my inner voice to share, I smoothly incorporated this into my holistic practice and began sharing my own process with others.

Channeling Jesus myself in recent years, I am always concerned about confusing His words with my own. Eventually I got used to the firm, but gentle, non-judgmental tone, and I would recognize the loving and concise dialogues as His. The messages were short and simple, and I understood them from some deep place within me. Compelling information flowed in, as if to briefly and gently touch the wisdom of my soul.

Usually, a source of guidance is one that is familiar, perhaps someone close to you, or, in my case and my mother's, Jesus. When I am outdoors, present to my surroundings, I may sense His message through the characteristics and movements of animals and birds, the patterns of landscape, or the qualities of water. The hawk flying high above me may be a reminder to focus on things from a higher perspective outside of the mind. From there, I know He is directing me to something important.

I have grown accustomed to His few, gentle reminders of what I already know in my heart. One message, which was initially puzzling, was that many of my clients and students teach in various fields. Interestingly, I came to realize that I was being called to educate teachers who could have a significant impact. What a clever plan to reach a vast audience. Was that Jesus' intention for me all along?

While preparing the move to Upstate New York, I awoke early one morning, and clearly heard a strong, firm, yet gentle voice say to me, "Tell him how you feel." I wanted to keep this voice hidden, knowing I was not being honest with myself about moving. My mind went quickly to supporting my husband, Jack, to move for his work. In my heart, I felt I would be leaving family, a business I just established, and friends, to go to an unknown place, which to me, was in the middle of nowhere.

Certainly, hearing those words, "Tell him how you feel," three consecutive times got my attention.

Despite knowing their importance, I remained true to my old pattern and quickly tucked the message away. I proceeded to pack my belongings because that is what my mind guided me to do. Looking back, had I told my husband exactly how this move was going to affect me, it would have been a smoother transition. I know he would have agreed. Never having experienced life outside this small corner of the world, moving was bound to affect my life. How was I to process that and my obligations at the same time? Like my mother, the ability to express my true feelings was a challenge.

With deep sadness, I compromised, knowing we would be located between Chicago and Boston to be somewhat near our families. Jack would continue his career, doing what he loves to do, and I could reestablish my business in the Rochester area.

Divine guidance has many ways of revealing itself. If we don't receive it one way, there will be another, more obvious cue. When we purchased our first house in New York, I was still unsettled. I had to learn where everything was and how to get there. I often argued with Jack, taking out my frustration on him when I got lost. Always in the back of my mind were those words, "Tell him how you feel," and there they would stay.

Finally, a family of deer was sent to me. When they camped out in the woods behind my house, I was not aware of the symbolism of their presence because I was simply looking for ways to hold onto my garden. My neighbors had all the methods and potions to steer them in another direction, however, nothing worked. Only later would I understand that they were there for me; their gentle and focused energy helped me gradually settle into this new environment. By the second year, those energies came more into balance within me, allowing my resistance to living here fade. The deer quietly and gradually drifted to a new home and garden.

Without realizing it, I was on a path to broaden my awareness, preparing myself for His teachings, and possibly discovering a new purpose. What Jesus asks of us will never be a sacrifice. However, it can be perceived that way. Losing someone close to us or anything of value can feel like an impossible hurdle to step over. If we are patient and understand the truth revealed behind that loss, we will see how it leads to the next gift of Spirit.

Whenever I act on Jesus's guidance, I am given everything I need—the strength, direction, and means to accomplish what is being asked. Although it feels right to follow His guidance, it is a bit scary because He only gives one step or prompt at a time. If I knew His full plan up front, I would never feel confident enough to achieve it. Staying in the moment and patiently trusting His steps, I have discovered that things fall perfectly into place with more ease and possibilities than I could imagine.

DECEMBER 31, 1982

"My dear ones, know that my ministry of prayer is the foundation of all my ministries. Prayer warriors are the front of every spirit battle. Kay and Fran, before you were, I have chosen you as prayer partners and prayer warriors." — Jesus

Finally, an explanation for why my mother and Aunt Kay were inseparable as far back as I can recall. Jesus certainly validates my observation that people often have an unexplainable instant connection, regardless of whether they are our children, parents, siblings, or friends. When these connections are nurtured, His broader plan is achieved.

Aunt Kay did not have children of her own and lived a mile down the street from our large family of eight. She loved spending time with us, always at our house, helping with meals, cleaning, laughing, and having secret conversations at the kitchen table with my mother. When we went camping, she would stay behind, again, cleaning, but this time leaving special gifts or notes on our beds. I was always excited when she did join us. I was her favorite until later conversations revealed my siblings claiming the same status.

Prayer was a big part of my mother and Kay's lives. They were devoted to the church and to the group. Although they were close because of their shared history, the plan had already been set before they incarnated here. I believe prayer helped them cope with many family and life situations. Although our family learned prayer, it was more meaningful for my mother and Aunt Kay.

Meditation and mindful practices have always brought stability into my life. Initially, prayer for me was about asking for material things; then later, asking to see things from a different perspective. As time passed, the role of 'prayer partners' in my life evolved, taking on a new meaning. Whenever I need it, there is always someone there to listen without judgment in my darkest moments. Healing often occurs simply through having the opportunity to express misdirected thoughts, seeing the truth of any situation, and making room for miracles.

DECEMBER 24, 1982

"For my children, dark days are coming soon and all who know me will know my protecting love." — Jesus

In many other entries not included in this book, Jesus teaches the group to trust his love. At each meeting, He speaks to them from a loving place, while He clearly prepares them for future events. He continued throughout the notebooks to acknowledge the individual difficulties they were having and encouraged them to turn each one over to Him. The nature of these problems was equally worthy of being liberated and entrusted to Jesus.

In the 1980s, my mother would have witnessed the Middle Eastern unrest reflecting the darker times prophesied by Jesus. Today it would include the COVID-19 pandemic, Russia's invasion of Ukraine, climate change, and seeing many systems that desperately need revamping. Personal and world events always reveal opportunities to address our fears and bring more clarity and understanding into our awareness. The global pause, brought about by the pandemic, served as an opportunity to stop and view our lives differently to make necessary changes. Life-altering events, whether or not we are directly involved, present an opportunity to face our personal fears as they arise—fear of dying, fear of losing freedom, fear of being alone, fear of being unsafe, fear of being attacked, or fear of not having enough. These are common fears which are deeply held in our collective consciousness.

During my first year in private practice, I worked with a client in Massachusetts who was consumed with watching news about battles or wars in other countries. He was not sleeping and had difficulty eating, so I asked him to take a vacation from the news. When I saw him next, both his sleep and anxiety level had improved. The time away or break from the news helped him realize the anxiety and guilt he held since his time in Vietnam. He had survived, but many in his unit had not.

This man was able to calm his own inner chaos long enough to hear the truth underneath the anxiety. His perception and reactions to events on the news changed, and he could cope better and see things differently. Peace naturally surrounded him while the intensity of his tragic story faded.

My mother had many opportunities at home to practice trust and let go of worries and fears. I can almost sense her response to recent global disasters. The rosary beads would be in the living room ready when needed and she would be prepared and reassuring. His protective love would have been known to her by this time in the same way I know how He supported me during the coronavirus pandemic.

Benefits are many when one relates to divine help, especially during difficult times. We are trained at an early age to keep a constant state of hyperalertness over the details of our life, and this seems to work temporarily. However, the way of Jesus is filled with more ease and grace. Lasting solutions and healing take place when we can accept His invitation to stillness and ask for that protective love.

It is my gradual trusting in Jesus and the many ways He sends messages that led me to depend on His love and protection, especially during challenging times. I receive much-needed information in many varied ways. Sometimes I hear His guiding words in different media, lyrics of a song, a conversation with someone, or simple directive words that come into my awareness.

DECEMBER 27, 1983

"Many of my children are unaware of the spirit battle raging around and about and within them. Many do not know that they can turn to me in perfect trust and be led by me. I will uphold you and strengthen and sustain you."

— Jesus

The reference Jesus makes to spirit battle is all too familiar. Time and time again my ego mind becomes unruly as it goes over every detail of the past and projects to the future with its fear. On August 20, 2020, I was attempting to meditate and noticed that my mind was distracted by uncomfortable symptoms in my body. My intent was to uncover more thoughts and beliefs that were causing these symptoms. Having done inner reflection for many years, it was frustrating to, again, be confronted with annoying body symptoms. How many layers of distressful thoughts are contained in one mind?

Following is my conversation with Jesus through a channeled message. I asked for His help in releasing these patterns and beliefs that keep me from moving forward.

Jesus: *Loved one, I am always here for you when you are ready to turn to me. It is that simple. Forget how to clear things as you do, just simply turn to me. Your answers lie in your choices.*

Me: *How can I turn away from things that seem so difficult and real in my experience?*

Jesus: *They are not real. They are manifestations of your thoughts. They replace Me.*

It is easy to lose sight of the simplicity of turning to Him. If we don't work hard at something, there is no good outcome. Over the years, He has patiently reminded me He is supporting my awakening and that unraveling the past needs time and patience. He has been clear that I am not the one to do the unraveling.

Residual fears from the past, triggered by the pandemic, soon emerged to cloud my thinking once again. One day, I remember pulling up to a parking space at my crowded local grocery store, watching others walk in confidently with their masks on. Not so self-assured, I inhaled deeply as I put on my mask. Was I ready to trust Spirit today and not fall victim to this virus?

Before I left the car, I asked Jesus for His guidance and protection. Entering through the least crowded side entrance, I stopped, puzzled. Immediately, I felt directed to the opposite side of the store, away from my usual shopping pattern. The guidance took me to a group of shoppers at the end of the paper goods aisle where a masked customer was happily handing out toilet paper. Grateful to receive this gift, I looked behind him to see only a few rolls left in the last box of the aisle. All I could do was smile under the cover of my required face mask.

Jesus continued to be with me as I navigated my cart down each aisle. Wherever I walked, people seemed to stay a suitable distance from me, as if there was something invisible around me that prevented anyone from getting closer. Moving through the store, I found everything I needed. There was a feeling of comfort and safety, which continued through standing in line at checkout with the essential six feet distance. I was in full trust surrounded by His strength; and as the pandemic continued, I realized more and more the power of just turning to Him and asking for help.

DECEMBER 27, 1982

"I give you my strength for my work. I am preparing you to walk my road, serve as I serve, and die to the world of flesh as I did. For then, and only then will you live in spirit, walking the earth." — Jesus

How does one live in spirit and walk the earth at the same time? Jesus knew He was more than his physical body. He knew He was supported during His mission here. He knew that to truly walk in the spirit of His Father, he had to know His own essence and shed light on any remaining doubt or conflict. The road He walked was the one we travel today that helps us release what we created from the ego, or the world of flesh, to find peace in the present. It is becoming more apparent than ever that we need to look beneath the ego-created life (the accomplishments and degrees) we have made to find our true purpose—remembering our divinity and remembering that with His help, there is nothing we can't do.

A whisper away, Jesus, the welcoming and unwavering One who knows our life plan, is always available waiting for us to ask for help while doing

His work. However, we rarely call upon the Spirit or Jesus for guidance. Eventually, as humans, we tire of doing things our way and finally give up the need to control our lives. Spirit loves that moment when our minds grow silent in defeat, because it is then that we can hear God's word and align with His mission for us. Jesus knew this was the way to join in ease once again with His Creator, not at death, but embodied here on earth.

I believe my mother, my aunt, and the other members of the group were part of a movement to plant seeds to show us the way back to Spirit. What if she had not sought this peaceful following? What would the members of our family be like today? What would my relationship be like with her today? Our past would not have come to a place of forgiveness. I would have held on tightly to my anger and stubbornness, keeping us in separation, and, if she did the same, I imagine I would have been devastated. Also, I may not have the same relationship with my siblings that I have today.

Despite the diversity of my mother's group, they fully committed to prayer and achieving personal inner peace with His guidance. Their light continues to shine to us in service, spreading much needed awareness.

"Mary is resting in me. I have allowed ill health that she may take time apart with me. Ruth Ann is running. Continue to pray for this tender-hearted child, for she is reaching a point of exhaustion."—Jesus

In this notebook entry, Mary, a member of the group, had an opportunity to rest as a reminder to slow down and connect with Jesus. Illness, unfortunately, was the vehicle for her to be still to observe her thoughts and discover what needed to change in her life. When I read this entry, I am reminded of the many times an event or illness required me to be still. As difficult as it was, I grew to accept these times as opportunities to heal my inner conflicting and unresolved thoughts that come to life during this time of rest. Rather than see this experience as a form of suffering, I know now that I can use the silence, feel what my soul is needing, and honor its request. I am always grateful to see the light and awareness at the end of that darkened tunnel.

Ruth Ann, another member of the group, was reaching a point of exhaustion. Running or busying ourselves is a useful strategy or avoidance behavior used to distract from the truth about any situation we want to avoid. In a flurry of tasks, we overlook the reality of unresolved fatigue, distressing thoughts, and hidden emotions. However, one reaches a point of intolerance or, as in her case, exhaustion.

I love the reminders from Jesus throughout the notebook entries that prompt me to turn over my struggles to Him. Peace and surprising miracles seem to follow in the wake of these self-nurturing moments.

Before my mother joined the charismatic group, her free time was limited. She only had moments to herself during visits with my Aunt Kay, when with other family members, while working in the garden, or during some brief periods of relaxation at the beach as we grew older. I believe Mom found some pleasure in her role in the home, but she was grateful to participate in the group. It offered her a much-needed pause and connection with her own needs.

"Remember always, I am the doer. I and I alone am the one who sees and does. You are my Instruments." —Jesus

My mother found comfort and healing in handing over the details of her life to Jesus. At first, I interpreted these actions as her disengaging from parenting. In all appearances, she was more peaceful, but I was more confused about her chosen silence. Later discoveries would, however, alter my interpretation.

Not understanding at the time that it was possible to ask for help, my life gradually became an endless list of things to do. Although I was intuitive about my surroundings, there was little connection to my spirit or my own needs. My spiritual practice was limited to swimming, sunbathing, and dancing. Although they were relaxing and freeing, something was still missing. Peace was fleeting at best.

I would later learn from *A Course in Miracles* that *"a healed mind does not plan. It carries out the plans that it receives through listening to wisdom that is not its own. It waits until it has been taught what should be done and then proceeds to do it. It does not depend upon itself for anything except its adequacy to fulfill the plans assigned to it. It is secure in certainty that obstacles cannot impede its progress to the accomplishment of any goal that serves the greater plan established for the good of everyone."*

Unfortunately, I grew up in a culture that believed plans, goals, and finishing something would keep me in good graces with the world; however, to me, plans and goals seemed out of reach, as survival was the main theme. The jobs I held taught me what I did not want. Looking back later, the unconscious knowing of what fed my soul helped me to realize that each position was a steppingstone to a much-needed inner soul search.

Experts have long known to take the word "should" out of our language because of its implication of duty and responsibility. Living in that state of obligation eventually became exhausting for my mother, and later, for me. Jesus said, *"I and I alone am the one who sees and does. You are my instrument."* It doesn't mean that we take no action. For me, it is an opportunity to pause, check in with how I feel about an action I am about to take, then listen for the guidance. With many later experiences of letting go of "doing" as an adult, I can see now how my mother needed to follow this same guidance to find her own personal peace.

Gradually, I became more attuned to asking for help in my life. One day, before going to the car dealer for a recall repair, I thought it would be an opportunity to consider a newer vehicle model. For a couple of years, I had been worried about my car's age and potential problems. As the time approached to take the car into the shop, I became acutely aware of never having made these purchase decisions alone. I spent the week educating myself to be better prepared... or "the doing," as Jesus said.

I left the house that morning with an open mind, deciding to call on Jesus to guide me. His response was for me to listen and look for all the guidance being presented. When I arrived for the recall, I asked the man at the front desk if the mechanic would evaluate the car for a trade-in. The mechanic asked why I wanted to spend money on a new car when the motor, transmission and tires were in great shape and the mileage was only 147,000. This model claimed to be reliable up to 300,000 miles. When I explained I travel long distances periodically, he told me to stop worrying.

Was this the sign Jesus was talking about? I was amazed at how unusual it was for someone in a dealership to actively discourage someone like me—a woman with scant knowledge of cars. When I left, I was puzzled, but later felt better knowing my car would be safe and dependable on the road for a while. Not emotionally ready to release my car then, I believed He would guide me when the time came, as cleverly as He helped me let go of worries about this visit to the dealer.

I marvel at how inner guidance and messages come as a gentle voice that does not seem like mine; yet it feels genuine, like a sense of just knowing that some place deep inside me holds the same wisdom.

"I am with you. Do not fear. My gift of knowledge is for the asking. Do not shut out your mind to my word. Be always alert to what is not mine. I am always with you. Fear keeps you from hearing my word." —Jesus

To me, the proclamation from Jesus, *"Fear keeps you from hearing my word,"* are an important point in this notebook entry. Fear is a dark wall of past and future thoughts that block out guidance of any kind. It is an overwhelming feeling that paralyzes. Once we take a breath and come back to the present moment, the fear weakens, and we open to the help in front of us and the reality that He is with us.

My mother showed much fear prior to her work with the charismatic group. I felt it often as she nervously allowed me to experience life. Not quite aware of when the shift occurred, I was grateful when her fears subsided.

Confronting my fears of starting college and the challenge of raising a child at the same time, I hesitated to enroll and kept coming up with excuses. However, on the day of registration, Ron, a close family friend, unexpectedly appeared at my doorstep. Given our earlier conversations, he must have sensed my hesitation, as he disregarded my doubts and the support crutches I required following a minor foot surgery. Standing in the doorway with an air of confidence, Ron seemed to see that my anxieties were obstructing my progress. I finally allowed myself to embrace the idea that he was trying to help me overcome them.

With a strong desire for education lying beneath my fear of the unknown and Ron's insistence on taking me to the college, I cautiously settled into a new chapter of my life. The pervasive fog of fear diminished as the strength of trust in my abilities grew.

I knew I was supported and on the right course for me. A neighbor generously offered to see my son off to school every morning and my family was there for him after school. I rode on a wave of energy I never knew I had. Nothing dissuaded me from learning as much as I could about medicine and how to help others. Looking beyond fear, I understood this was the way Jesus prevailed through my mother's prayers. She knew it was Him making the difference for me.

Although our family teased Mom, she attended her charismatic group meetings quietly. She knew in her heart this was the right place for herself.

Once my mother and I were able to release our individual doubts and fears, we could more easily follow divine guidance; my mother from Jesus, and me from an inner voice I did not understand at the time . Even though I could not sense Him at the time, I believe Jesus was with both my mother and me, beautifully orchestrating the intricate details of our unique paths.

JANUARY 3, 1983

"Only through intimate prayer will I reveal my plans for each one." — Jesus

Again, Jesus is calling us to be still to hear His guidance and plan. My mother frequently went into prayer and followed the voice that ultimately led her to find peace. When I saw her resting in the afternoon on the sofa in the living room, shades partially down, I always thought she was recovering from the day. Now I know there was much more occurring. Perhaps Jesus was in the room with her.

Intimate prayer with Jesus is simple. We don't need to ask for specifics, but to ask to see things differently when we are feeling upset about the way we are currently viewing a problem. We do not need a formal altar or a place in the world that is more sacred than another. He is in our hearts, ready and waiting for us to allow His support. Once we ask, it is important to look for the ways He responds. The answers lie within us.

I believe my mother looked forward to knowing the next step of His plan for her, as I do now for me. Again, I imagine her entering the wide, welcoming wooden doors of a church and dropping the roles she played as a mother and wife. There was respite from the worry and mundane tasks as she entered the space she considered so sacred, peaceful, and nurturing to her soul.

JANUARY 3, 1983

"The treasures of the kingdom are yours, all at your request. You have only to ask in order to receive. Ask what is in the will of God and receive in abundance. Continue to lift your families to me. I have much love to give them. They will share in the abundance in my everlasting love for you. Know this and go forth." — Jesus

As infinite souls, we are abundant in time, resources, health, help, love, and more. *A Course in Miracles* teaches us to ask for the remembrance of who we are because that knowledge will open us to seeing the abundance around us. We already have everything we need. The question is, are we ready to receive these long forgotten treasures that have been hidden under the shadow of our thoughts?

It is easy to mistrust when we have our own perception of how or when we experience the effortless flow of abundance. Abundance is blocked when we believe it cannot come until we have worked very hard or have done something to earn it. Often, we don't see the abundance around us when we have limited ideas of what it should look like.

One may see the loss of a job, while another sees an abundance of time.

I need to remind myself often to ask for God's will, as He knows the best plan and its infinite possibilities more than I could ever imagine. His gentle response to prayer always arrives in divine timing and from a place of love. He continues to remind us to lift others to Him.

JANUARY 3, 1983

"Margarette is mine. She is bound with a spirit of self-pity and resentment. Pray and I will set her free. Margarette must grow in spirit. Share with her my love, but do not coddle her, for she will not lean on me if she continues to lean on her friends. She feels left out. She knows not that none other has more opportunity to share with me than she has. Her doubts are self-made, and she can't overcome them until she frees herself of self-pity. She must be willing to fight the battle, each has a battle, and each has her own place in the arena of Jesus. Children, each must perform his own work, each one must be a friend to one another, but no one can do the work assigned to one and manage to do the work assigned to themselves if the work is to be well done in My name. Then each carries his own weapon, each must be in his own place, each must depend on me as the leader of the army of God. No one else is called to carry the gear of another. Remember, do your part and be willing to help another in prayer and sacrifice. No one can live the life of another. Each must walk his lonely path. Go now and ponder my word." — Jesus

Margarette, another member of the group, is being held in love while she goes through her own dark moment. Despite the support the group is willing to give her, Jesus is saying that it is time for them to let go. This will give Margarette a new experience of focusing on all the things that hold her back from knowing who she really is beyond her self-pity.

Although this is a long notebook entry, I feel compelled to include it because it clearly speaks for itself. What better opportunity to avoid our own problems than to step in and coddle another? If someone is in a space of self-pity, it is easy to commiserate with them if we are deeply feeling another's pain. When we are in this place, we only bring our weakness to others. We may not see the friend improve and, eventually, we become resentful of the time we have distracted ourselves from our own lives.

Placing others first at the expense of our own needs can be exhausting. My mother must have reached that breaking point after years of devotion to our family. She knew when it was time to absorb His teachings.

In my own experience, I enabled someone who was not committed to letting go of their painful past story. At times, the effort spent did not change the outcome of their situation and I was left disappointed, wondering what I could have done better. Jesus is clear that *no one is called to carry the gear of another.* I noticed when I follow this guidance and step back, I am clear about what is most helpful. Possibly then, I can see their situation differently and join with them in a more centered way or simply listen without judgment or attempting to fix anything. With plenty of occasions to practice, over time, I discovered this way is always more successful in the healing process.

Part 2

My Journey

Chapter Five

I grew up in a family strongly influenced by the teachings of the Catholic Church. There was always a picture of Jesus on the wall in the kitchen looking over our family. His eyes were loving and welcoming as they gazed at us in His soft, kind, way. It was uncomfortable for me to experience an expression so direct and attentive, but it was far more appealing and life-affirming than the image of suffering and crucifixion seen in the church. This contrast in images was just another confusing message to me. I was bursting with questions, but was never sure what or when to ask.

My mother was the keystone who held the strong tradition and faith in Jesus. Besides the kitchen picture, you could find a few bibles, a cross over a bed or two, and a pair of rosary beads laid carefully on an end table. Mom's daily worship was more private, saying the rosary for one reason or another in the living room or upstairs in her room. My mother prayed for me and my five siblings collectively or singularly, over the years. For me, I am sure it was necessary every time I walked out of the house. I didn't understand the value of her prayers then; however, I believe I grew up protected by her many sincere appeals to Jesus.

Often, I was torn between the messages of my religious faith and the feeling I had when entering the quiet sanctuary of a church. It became clear that what I so desperately needed was a sacred haven where I could connect with my own secret thoughts. Not knowing any other way to get that peace, I silently participated at mass.

Despite my father's similar religious background, I am not quite sure what his role was in the church during our upbringing. I suspect he simply followed my mother's lead while keeping his own faith private. He took us to church every Sunday or Christian holiday unless someone was ill. When that was the case, one of my parents would stay home with that child and the other parent would take the rest of us to mass.

Attending church was such a constant in our family that it did not stop during vacations. With a month off each year in August, my father took us camping for three weeks as a time for the family to be together or simply to keep us occupied.

I have only felt my father's presence a few times since he passed away in 1994. On one of those occasions, I was stirring the contents of dinner on the stove and suddenly I experienced a powerful scent of pine and campfire. Curiosity gave way to a peaceful reminder of him on those vacation adventures. Later, I shared this moment with my cousin, Cathy, who was visiting for the weekend. During a moment in the backyard, we realized that the discussion of my father's presence led my cousin to see her father in a different, more positive light.

For each camping trip to western Massachusetts and sometimes a visit to family in Nova Scotia, packing everything but the kitchen sink began two weeks prior. Besides camping gear, my mother packed full dress outfits for each of us to attend church, complete with dresses, hats, white gloves, polished shoes, and one not so complicated outfit for my brother. I quietly tolerated this because the rest of the vacation we spent enjoying the outdoors and allowing nature to absorb and transform our huge family energy.

My siblings and I were baptized as infants and later received the sacraments of first communion and confirmation as a way of strengthening faith in the church as my parents did. With no smile or expression on my face, my communion picture was a serious portrait of me at eight-years-old, my hands in prayer position at my heart, sitting still, as I was probably told.

Catechism classes to prepare for receiving confirmation continued to reinforce my mood of unhappiness. I unknowingly longed for a calm discussion about the meaning of faith. The priest was such a strict teacher; it was difficult for me to sit through each class or to grasp the sacraments. Frequently, for fear of doing something wrong, I would grow tense as the watchful priest reinforced my unrest. He walked up and down the aisles and randomly slammed his ruler down on the hard surface of our wooden desks.

My mother was aware of the priest's authoritarian practices in catechism class. She joined with others in the church to have him removed. When that failed, she went to a neighboring church requesting our family be transferred, only to be told we could not continue classes outside of our town. The priest was eventually removed, but not before we were confirmed and not in time to erase his harsh, lingering imprint.

Although I generally disliked mass, there was a period in the 1950s and early 1960s when I found it captivating. During this time, Latin was spoken or sung in the church. The beauty of this language filled the air, mingling with the scent of incense in a church characterized by its lofty ceilings and a dim interior, the latter a result of the rich, deep colors of the stained-glass windows. I was enchanted by the ceremonies that the priests conducted in this foreign tongue. The gentle sounds of the organ playing in the background added to the grandeur of the ritual. It was an escape from the annoyances of school and home. My lack of understanding of Latin didn't hinder the experience; instead, the melodic nature of the language led me into a state of deep peace.

Later, it became difficult to contain my confused thoughts. When I could freely travel alone to church during high school, I noticed that those unspoken thoughts often brewed to a raging storm of anger and rebellion. I sat at the back of the church for quick escapes, skipped masses to be with my friends, fought with everyone in the house, and spent my time outside as much as I could. I felt unsettled and immersed myself in friendships and relationships away from home.

As a young adult, I cautiously maintained the familiar faith and sporadically attended masses on Sundays. There were enough experiences through parenting, college, and relationships to keep my soul searching, never giving up the need to understand more about life with or without a formal religion. Although my mother was not happy with my on again, off again commitment to the church, she interfered less and less.

One of the most important realizations I embraced over the years was to accept things as they were in the church because I knew the only one I could change was myself. As I focused attention on those eventual changes, anger toward the ways of the church subsided and my mind was clearer to hear my own voice and inner guidance. Harsh characteristics in the church eventually changed with an increase in public awareness, giving some of my younger siblings and my son a more welcoming experience.

Chapter Six

There have been many experiences outside the structure of a church that encouraged my faith and trust in something beyond my understanding. One of them happened in my late twenties driving to visit my mother and Aunt Kay. Absorbing the warm summer breeze through the open window, I arrived at the familiar bridge close to our family home when something flew in the driver's window and hit my left eye. Simultaneously, the bridge went up over the inlet, stopping traffic. The stinging pain and watering increased as I sat waiting.

When I finally arrived at the house, I raced through the front door onto the enclosed porch, making all the noise I could muster. My mother and Aunt Kay were at the kitchen table, the one place I knew I would find them. They both stood to see what was causing the commotion. Concerned, Mom looked in my eye, pulled the lid up and down, searching silently for the object that was causing so much distress. My heart was racing as I stood patiently in their care. Aunt Kay stood behind me and placed a comforting hand on my shoulder. Immediately on sensing the touch of her hand, the pain disappeared. Mom really saw nothing in my eye and did nothing except to look. When calmness came over my body, they both stepped back from me. I noticed how they exchanged a knowing smile, sharing something secret between them that would stay that way. This was a miracle I did not easily understand and one they both knew I was not ready to hear. Was it silent prayers or their loving presence and their strong faith that cured my pain? All of it was beyond my comprehension. I went to the mirror and saw no redness around or in my eye, which would be typical of that much irritation.

The next event to draw me closer to the miraculous was on December 20, 1984. It was a clear, sunny winter morning with remnants of past snow accumulation. I was on Christmas break, excited to be free from classes and have time to join my long-time friend, Duane, who was in town for Christmas. Since my son was twelve, our first task, of course, was shopping. I drove to pick up Duane, gladly tossed him the car keys, and relaxed in the passenger seat. Thinking about the day ahead, he hesitantly left his little Maltese dog behind.

Our day began early, with stores open at 8:00am to accommodate last-minute shoppers. We started in Hanover on Route 18 at The Toy Box. Lists in hand, we quickly got in and out of this store. As I placed our purchases in the trunk, I noticed that I was taking longer than usual, meticulously straightening and organizing, even though I had been in a hurry just moments before. When Duane asked why I was taking so long, I couldn't explain. It simply felt like time was slowing down. Back in the car, we drove north toward the next store. Knowing we were making good progress and I didn't have to drive, I eagerly took this opportunity to unwind from the stress of school and let my eyes wander away from the road in front of me. I daydreamed as I looked out the passenger window at the many stores and businesses decorated for the holidays.

As we traveled on this busy two-lane road, my attention was suddenly brought to the blunt force of Duane's protective arm across my chest. Words never had a chance to express what I saw, and I only recall a blur of gray across the windshield–then silence.

Traveling too fast and trying to avoid hitting the car in front of him, the driver of a large commercial dump truck swerved into our lane, hitting us head on.

After slipping in and out of consciousness, I eventually realized we had been in an accident. Duane called out to me in a weak, gentle, and what seemed like a distant voice. The natural endorphins released in my body protected me from feeling pain. In this space and time, everything became surreal; I was unaware of the need to move my body, and I felt no sense of urgency to do anything but check on Duane. Sometime later, I was relieved to hear the distant sounds of many rescue vehicles.

Soon, I became aware of the piercing sounds of extrication equipment. Attempting to look around and get my bearings, I realized Duane was not responding at all now. Terrified, I yelled out into a darkness that clouded my vision.

My pleading words drew the first responder to me, who explained he had taped my eyes shut because of a laceration over my eyelid. At that point, he tried to stay as close as possible, reassuring me with frequent updates. My training as an Emergency Medical Technician and nursing student did not prepare me to be the one needing help. Instead, my awareness was heightened knowing everything the responders were doing and why. Their conversation told me the car's frame was buckled under the driver's side, with the steering wheel jammed against Duane's chest. As I struggled to sit up, the paramedic attempted to calm my fear. Distressed by not hearing Duane's response, I found myself unable to follow even the simplest instructions from the paramedic.

The ear-piercing sound of the machinery typically used in these sorts of accidents told me all I needed to know and did not want to hear. The damage was severe, and rescuers had difficulty getting Duane out of the car. It would take another hour before he would be free. Realizing I was being moved from the front passenger floor onto a backboard, I began to panic. They were preparing to realign my right hip quickly, a procedure that, although brief, felt intense. The deafening sounds of the equipment faded as the rescue truck transferred me to the hospital.

We were badly injured, but amazingly, we were alive. When Duane finally arrived at the same emergency room, they placed him in a bed just beyond the open curtain next to me. His face was swollen, and he had a cervical collar around his neck. I was astonished he could smile in response to me. However, within minutes, he stopped communicating entirely.

I immediately alerted the staff, who then swiftly closed the curtain to separate us. Unsure of the extent of his injuries, they were planning to do more tests and move him to the operating room. I waited anxiously. My injuries seemed trivial in comparison.

Hours went by before the Chief of Plastic Surgery, whom I was promised was worth the wait, arrived to patiently remove the embedded shards of glass from my forehead. It was only then that I realized my foot was badly sprained as I struggled to move my leg. Little did I know that this injury would dramatically change the course of my career and my view of alternative medicine.

That night, Duane's floor nurse helped him to place a call to my room, intending to give me an update. He narrated how he was taken to the operating room and, prior to any actual procedure, he woke to a light above his head. He asked the surgeon, half-jokingly, if that was THE light and I was pleased he had not lost his sense of humor. But the surgeon was not amused. He continued to prepare for surgery, looking over what appeared to be normal imaging and laboratory test results. Puzzled, he wanted to know what Duane was made of, because what happened to us was like hitting an oak tree at high speed. As he double-checked the results and re-examined Duane, he then wanted to know who was watching over him. Shaking his head in disbelief, the surgeon removed his gloves and left the room. Duane needed neither the doctor nor the procedure.

Across town, my mother and Aunt Kay were finishing a group meeting at church. My mother was almost out the door when she saw my aunt stop and turn to light another candle. Having already lit candles as part of their group offering, my mother was confused. Aunt Kay disregarded my mother's attempts to move her along and continued to light the candle. The time was 9:20am, the exact time of our car accident. When I heard this later, I recognized it was another miracle that, like my eye healing, I could not ignore and another mystery I did not understand but accepted. My mother kept her thoughts to herself out of respect, knowing I was not yet open to the idea of divine intervention.

While on the mend, I needed to make many adjustments to care for my son and get him back to school. I did not feel the presence of Jesus at this time, nor could I understand why or how we had survived. With that mystery tucked safely away in the cluelessness of my mind, I went on to recover from injuries and begin an intense schedule at school, physical therapy, and home. Lying on the floor at the end of every day to alleviate the headaches and back discomfort got me through dinner and my homework schedule. No longer could I study until 1:00am and get up comfortably at 6:00am.

When I shared my mother's story with Duane, he seemed to understand the meaning behind prayer and my Aunt Kay's need to light the candle at the exact time of our accident. He strongly believed that the prayer or intention she set by lighting the candle had something to do with our survival. Perhaps my aunt responded to inner guidance that led her to know if or when it was time to light the second candle.

I had grown up learning how to pray, but I did not fully understand how prayers were answered. Yet it was hard to dismiss the fact that my cousin, who was also going to come with us that day, and Duane's Maltese dog were not part of the divine plan at the last minute.

Despite our injuries, we both supported each other as we continued to heal. Duane decided to stay in Massachusetts until he fully recovered from a concussion. For me, clinic rotations in the hospital were delayed, but I could return to the college classroom in February and finally graduate at the end of 1986.

Over the years, we have kept our miracle alive, believing there are no accidents, only moments of awareness of God's presence. Although it was not the ideal way to alter my career goals, the accident provided many opportunities to explore a diverse path that eventually would lead me to complementary medicine. I believe Duane and I received the most precious of Christmas gifts that year.

Chapter Seven

It wasn't until 2008 that I experienced an event that gave me a direct encounter with Jesus. Accompanying my friend Gerri, one Sunday morning and curious to learn about different services, we explored a local church in the city. The church she found had a relaxed feeling to it, unlike the reserved, somber atmosphere I often felt entering my childhood church. These members expressed their excitement openly at seeing each other with lots of hugging. The sermon spoke to everyday situations and challenges in a kind, loving way, and there was upbeat music performed by a live band. We eagerly stood up to join in the singing. The repetitive words and inspiring lyrics were simple enough to follow. Soon, while the singing went on, I abruptly stopped, feeling somewhat confused. This happened as the band members each raised one hand towards the sky whenever God's name was mentioned. Surprised by this gesture and puzzled by my reaction, I remained standing and simply listened.

As the song neared the end, I felt a powerful presence in the empty seat next to me. I recognized the light-filled image to be that of Jesus, as I know Him from pictures I'd seen in my childhood. Here, He was clothed in a loose white robe with his left hand over his heart. The message was clear, "God is right here." It was a profound moment of knowing that He is not in the sky out of our reach. He is right here in our hearts. This message resonated so deeply for me, and I felt an immense wave of relief. When the music stopped, I fell back into the chair, trying to fully absorb all that had happened in these few short minutes.

Memories of my childhood years flooded my mind. Jesus or God was always depicted as someone far away, unapproachable, and possibly someone to fear. But here He was in a loving presence.

Overwhelmed by this experience, I began doubting myself. Did this just happen? At the same time, I was humbled and wondered why He would appear to me and why He would come with a loving reminder of what I somehow knew deeply within the core of my being, but had simply forgotten.

I wanted so badly to share this news with my mother. I was ready to burst forth with my new discovery—knowing she would be ecstatic to hear it. Sadly, this was not to be; she had passed away the year before.

Instead, I told Gerri what happened on our walk to the car. Fascinated, she wanted every detail of this miracle because, after her father passed away, it wasn't Jesus, but her father who came to her in the same way when she needed help.

Gerri did not stop searching for her ideal church. So weeks later, I went along again for the ride. Entering the new church, not quite knowing what to expect, we chose to sit in the back for an easy escape. The minister began his sermon, which related to common day-to-day challenges. As he proceeded, his voice gradually became louder and louder until his words shattered the silence and peace of this sacred room we had entered just moments before. I noticed my heart rate increasing and my palms sweat. Remembering the angry sermons growing up, one thing was clear: I had a choice of what to accept. "Three more minutes and I need to leave," I whispered, turning to Gerri beside me, who understood immediately.

What happened next amazed me. This time, Jesus appeared directly in front of me, but facing the minister. His long robe and outstretched arms shielded me from this intense sermon. With such gratitude for His presence, I closed my eyes and felt myself lean into Him. Relieved, I inhaled deeply and felt my anxiety melt with each tired breath. Within a brief time, the minister lowered his voice in the same manner a nob would lower the volume on a stereo.

Later, I learned that the appearances of Jesus were preparing me for an even deeper experience by slowly building my trust. Again, He only told me what I already knew, and He simply offered the awareness and permission to make another choice. He seemed to be on a mission to increase my awareness of those familiar intuitive "gut" feelings that have served me throughout the years.

I believe my openness to Him and my thirst for a deeper understanding of myself were an invitation to accept His guidance more clearly and consistently. It was the beginning of a deeper experience of turning to Him as my life unfolded.

Chapter Eight

In 2015, this loving Ascended Master, Jesus, came to me again, appearing in the stillness of my winter morning walks. With just a glance or the few words He spoke, I experienced a sensation that guided me to look at a memory or behavior pattern that drained my energy—self-judgment, following logic instead of feeling, or putting others first. These encounters from January through April happened weekly, sometimes daily.

I did not summon Jesus, nor was I thinking of Him, yet I welcomed His frequent visits. Beginning a walk with a simple question in my mind, such as, "What do I need to know next?" or "Help me see this situation differently," usually led to His appearance with a powerful, loving response.

In His familiar soft image, the robe now tied at the waist, He would stroll at my left side with hands clasped behind His back, the way one would walk in a casual, pondering manner. Occasionally, He would appear directly in front of me in a more formal and serious stance.

One time, I stopped walking, overcome with a strong emotion that surged into my experience. What followed was the awareness of long-held memories begging to be liberated. I was shocked at my reaction and the tears that followed. Yet I was also delighted and relieved that His patient presence was all I needed to let go of something that had unknowingly interfered with my desire to move forward.

When Jesus verbally expressed Himself, I clearly differentiated His use of the English language from mine. He used only a phrase, a single word, or simply His divine essence to echo volumes of meaning. The tone of His message was strong, loving, and always direct.

My mother never described an experience of seeing Jesus visually. I know guidance came to her through the verbal language of Tongues and prayer. Either way, she received similar profound messages for herself and the group as I receive in my meditation and walks today.

The visits from Jesus that winter served to accelerate my path to self-realization. His guidance shifted my perception of my life experiences and my level of consciousness. Already on a path of raising my awareness since the 1980s, and more intensely since 2003, I was not a stranger to inner reflection. I welcomed my new teacher.

I realized later that I had received moments of guidance long before Jesus began His winter lessons with me. For example, during my first year in nursing school, I heard His quiet moments of guidance through my nursing instructors as they reiterated similar messages. They taught us that one of the most important things to remember in our caring for patients was to enter their room only after having taken care of all our basic needs such as eating, drinking, and going to the restroom. We were also taught to keep our minds clear and open for the patients; this meant that we resolved any personal distractions or put them aside before arriving at the hospital each day. The instructor was not only teaching us to be present with the patients, but to take care of ourselves to improve the quality of our time with them. This was certainly similar to the core teachings to the group recorded in my mother's notebooks.

The instructor wasted no time showing us. At break time one day, twenty students lined up to share two restrooms. She moved herself right up to the front of the line, stood patiently waiting for the door to open, and scooted right in. I remember standing in that long line thinking, "How rude, but good for her!" She was taking care of herself as she taught us. When I discovered later that she was a mother of eight boys, it made more sense that she would have needed to develop that behavior. Even though this was a poor gesture on her part, it made me aware of all the times, past and present, that I put others before my own basic needs, as my mother did. Jesus would later help me as He did with the group, to unravel my need to put others first. Eventually, I embraced being present to myself first without distractions. Then it was easier to be of service to patients and others in my life. My intuition developed over time with this practice.

At graduation, another instructor had a similar message of self-care. The words, "Don't forget to play the piano," emphasized the need to make room for our passions no matter what path we take. This final departing wisdom helped me through the years that followed.

The words said that day helped me to remember how my mother sacrificed her passions. In our teens, my siblings and I discovered a box of Mom's artwork, sadly relegated to the attic storage. It contained a book on how to draw horses accompanied by her lifelike reproductions and cartoons. It was clear my mother had set aside an artistic talent to raise her children.

Art was an example of how my mother shelved what, at one time, had brought her joy. She held things close and private, allowing only a small part of herself to be revealed when someone in the family needed help, with not only art, but sewing or swimming. However, despite the decision to keep her talents hidden, the entire family grew to embrace our individual artistic gifts, which have emerged in many creative ways, and ones we all enjoy in each other today.

My favorite memory was when my son, Jason, came home from a summer art program with a colorful replication of Minnie and Mickey Mouse. I glanced over at my neighbor and friend, Shirley, who had also sent her son to summer school. She was thinking the same thing...we sent them because all we wanted during those summer mornings was some quiet time on the porch with our coffee. We also wanted to be confident they would not be hiding behind the bushes, camouflaged, to eavesdrop on our conversations. But there they stood with wide grins, revealing talents neither of us expected.

Chapter Nine

Growing up in the Catholic Church, my siblings and I learned at an early age that we were required to receive the Sacrament of Confession. Here we revealed our sins before we could kneel at the altar to receive the Communion wafer during Sunday mass.

As a child, I always felt fearful of what to say or what would happen if there was nothing to say to the priest waiting for my confession in the darkened booth. When I entered the church, the confessional booths were against the side wall. I would wait on the nearby pew until it was my turn to enter. Once inside, I knelt on one side of the booth facing a thick brown screen in silent, anxious anticipation of it sliding open. When it did, I barely saw the outline of the priest. I had a well-rehearsed list of sins, drawing from the many times I fought with my siblings about anything from clothes to bathroom space, or using profane language. The cycle of confession every month and communion on Sunday determined our lives. Each one seemed to come up quickly, one after the other. I rarely felt expressing my sins in this manner was useful. Today, I think a face-to-face conversation would have felt more supportive, and perhaps a better understanding of my anger would have emerged. My search for knowledge continued.

As Mom aged into her mid seventies, she was not consistent in going to confession. I was puzzled, but she never explained to me why she went less frequently. I recall taking her to a mass where we both kneeled at the altar to receive communion. My mother was a well-known parishioner, but I was a stranger to the congregation by this time. The older priest saw her and, with the host already in hand, he hesitated, then asked when she last went to confession. Mom dismissed him with one practiced, hardened look—a look I knew well. Not wanting to confront her during mass, the priest gave her the communion wafer and turned to the next person. I thought to myself, good for her! She had spent her life dedicated to the church. When we got to the car, we discussed the ridiculousness of his question.

My mother was certainly relaxing in the practice of her faith as she got older. With all the earlier rules of the church, it was time for her to ease the pressure she had put on herself to show her faith publicly, as well as getting us through all the church rituals expected of us. Had she come to the understanding that her private prayer was enough? Did she feel the formalities were no longer important? Did she get closer to sensing that Jesus only sees perfection in us?

Chapter Ten

On June 20, 1965, we learned that Pa, my paternal grandfather, passed away in the middle of the night. The kids, awakened by the hallway light, were asked to stay in their rooms to keep out of the way. All I heard were the whispered sounds of my parents as they made the necessary phone calls to my aunts and uncles. I was twelve years old at the time and did not understand death, nor did I understand all the secrecy.

What I did know was that my grandfather stood at the foot of my bed, looking as I remembered him — a gentle, soft-spoken man — but in a shadowy way. As he gazed at me, I froze in the confusion between what my parents had told me and what I saw. Although he uttered no verbal message, today I would say he conveyed to me he never really left in the way we understand death.

There was no one to share this experience with. My parents were intensely occupied, and I would not have known then how to explain this to my siblings.

The day my grandfather passed away and appeared to me in spirit, I couldn't fully trust what I saw. So, I suppressed the memory of his visit. However, thirty years later, during meditation, this memory resurfaced. He appeared again, but this time with a clear message: he wished to help our family from the other side, perhaps in a way similar to an angelic helper, a role he seemed to embrace willingly.

This encounter with Pa led to many more spiritual encounters with him and with others who had transitioned. I became confident not only in my deep desire to connect to the other side but also that I could indeed receive and understand these wise messages.

I recall a particular encounter connecting to my friend Shirley, who had passed years earlier. My grandsons were visiting me in Rochester. Halfway through the week, their fiery play with each other intensified, so I sent them outside to break up their loud, silly energy. Before I could face them again, I stood in the middle of the kitchen, discouraged, and yelled out to Shirley, "You should be here helping me raise these kids!" At that moment, my heart ached from the tremendous pain and reality of her absence. As I quieted my emotions, the room became still, and I heard her gently respond to my distress, whispering, "You always did the outdoors better." She was right. When things got too loud, playing outside with children always made me feel calmer, as I did not have to keep enforcing the house rules, and certainly their passionate energy was then put to better use. Feeling more grounded, I was ready to join them in the yard to play with whatever ball they were tossing.

My mother never described to me a direct visual experience with the other side. I know guidance came to her through the Catholic faith she knew so well, the language of Tongues, and daily prayer. Nevertheless, we know she received similar profound messages, as described in her notebooks, for herself and the group.

Chapter Eleven

It was the spring of 2019, and time again to make a trip back home. As usual, I loaded the car with much more than I needed—birthday presents for two of my three grandsons—and a lot of anticipation.

The previous summer, my son, Jason, had experienced a life-threatening health crisis that almost took him to death's door. Near the end of my week-long visit in late July, he mentioned feeling that something was not right in his body. Following a quick assessment, I became concerned and suggested he go to the emergency room. There, he was admitted to the ICU with an extensive and complex mix of three major infections.

My amazing family spent a month by his side helping me make tough decisions. For the next month, we were all focused on what his body was doing or not doing. Medical problems dominated most of our thoughts and conversations as we were caught up in the endless uncertainty of knowing too much or not enough.

While collaborating with my family and the doctors during Jason's hospital stay, I grappled with a whirlwind of volatile emotions that were especially extreme for me. The intensity of these events was so overwhelming that it left little room to stay connected to Jason's true Spirit or my own. One moment, I was trying to understand the full scope of what was happening; the next, I was sinking into an abyss of fear and grief. Often, I needed to step away to the waiting area, go outside for air, or retreat to my sister Mary's house for a moment of respite, much like my mother might have done when faced with a situation beyond her control. She used prayer and rosary in her time while I relied on meditation and meltdowns. Each time I felt my fear subside, I welcomed the release of cleansing tears that would eventually fade, bringing me a renewed strength to face the next moment.

Finally able to comprehend the broader situation, I realized how my emotions stood in the way of healing for both Jason and me. I stepped out into the waiting room more often to calm my emotions long enough to breathe and regroup.

Returning to Jason's room after releasing my cloud of fear, it was clear there was a miracle at work. A different clinical picture emerged showing he was improving in small ways—seeing him in a more restful state, needing less oxygen support, or getting confirming information from the doctors.

A crucial moment occurred when I entered the welcoming coolness of the hospital lobby on one ninety degree morning. Jason had been in the ICU for almost a month. Nearing the elevator, I suddenly turned and went back to the lobby. I sat in one of the chairs and simply could not control my emotions—I did not want to go back to that ICU!

It took the calming words of my patient friend, Tom, for me to muster the courage to walk back through those halls to see Jason. Two hours later, I dried my tears, took a deep breath, and arrived at the ICU somewhat ready to face the next moment. I was shocked to see that he had been admitted to a stepdown unit.

Entering Jason's new room and seeing him sitting up in a chair was beyond my comprehension. With his hands on my shoulders, Tom literally had to orient me to the reality of that moment as I heard Jason clearly say, "Hi Mom," for the first time in a month. It was amazing and relieving to witness this miracle unfold so quickly after releasing my many varied emotions in the lobby. This dramatic, amazing, and blessed change in his condition was a major step toward his healing and eventually leaving the hospital.

I remained in Boston until it was clear Jason continued to improve every day and plans for rehabilitation were in place. Even then, I was nervous about leaving, but my body demanded rest—I was depleted mentally, emotionally, and physically. The necessary decision to return home was finally made when I reached a point where it was obvious I could not absorb any more information. With lack of sleep and my exhausted mental state, it was time for me to step back and restore. I was concerned about the three-hundred-and-eighty-mile drive, so my ex-husband, Jack, agreed to lead me back when it was time to return to Rochester.

On my next trip to Boston months later, alone in the car, I was deep in thought, filled with worry and concern for my son. Although he was home and still recovering, random flashes of moments spent in the ICU still ran relentlessly through my mind. When not consumed by that, I relived his calls to me about multiple visits to various specialists, wondering whether I had considered everything or what the next course of action was. Doubts continually passed through my mind.

Before long, this mental chatter was interrupted by the appearance of a faded image of Jesus. His face appeared to the left of my steering wheel. His eyes were big and wide and held the brightest light I have ever seen, one even brighter than the picture of Him in my family home. It was not blinding, thank goodness, as I was traveling at highway speed. Then I clearly heard Him say, "See him through My eyes." I realized right away that I was not seeing Jason as he really is... motivated, determined, and strong. He knew what he wanted, and he was not sitting still for this. I needed to remember Jesus always sees us in the light of who we really are, which is beyond limitations of the body and certainly apart from how we perceive ourselves in judgment.

While embracing this message from Jesus, my reactions to Jason's condition slowly changed. I shifted my thinking away from problem-solving and more towards seeing this situation from a higher perspective with all its insights and lessons divinely timed. From there, evolved a deeper, more profound understanding of how Jesus sees us.

Jason was a big influence in helping me to let go of my pattern of worry. In response to one of my relentless parenting and medical questions, my son told me one day over the phone, "Before I tell you what the doctor said, I need you to know that I'm okay with this." At that moment, everything changed for me. I understood at a deeper level that I could not fix this situation, but I could only change my reactions. Accepting my son's need to make his own decisions, I trusted he would be guided every step of the way as I am. Jason survived this long, terrifying event for a reason. For me, it taught me to let go and trust, much the same way my mother trusted Jesus enough to let go of me.

As Jason kept healing, finding his bearings, and adjusting his lifestyle, his acceptance of the changes facing him renewed and strengthened my faith in his resilience. Finally I saw him without the veil of fear, as Jesus, with His pure thoughts, would see him. I can only imagine what my mother experienced when she discovered such a gift of setting worry aside to see things in a different light. I believe this is the place we both could relax and be the mothers we needed to be.

There was a reason the notebooks were left in my care to read.

Chapter Twelve

"Oh, my Jesus, I take this talk and give it up to you. I put my complete trust in you." – Frances, my mother

It was twelve noon in the early weeks of April 2016 and eight years after my mother passed. As I sat transcribing the last messages from the notebooks, I discovered four separate folded typed pages behind the last entry. The typing captured my attention immediately because all the material in the notebooks, so far, had been in my mother's handwriting. But here in my hands were pages of neatly typed words from our old familiar manual typewriter. Fascinated, I skimmed the pages to confirm my mother as the typist. The content appeared to be the draft of a talk she was to present to a group of people receiving the Sacrament of Baptism, which is part of the charismatic renewal. Excited about learning a new aspect of my mother's life, I placed the pages into my bag, anticipating a quiet time to review this new discovery.

Hours later, with time to explore the new pages, I settled into a chair in my healing room at the office. I was quickly drawn into my mother's personal thoughts that prepared her for the ceremony. Hearing her voice in my mind, the few words she used to describe her vulnerability as a mother took my breath away. Words she could never say at home lit up the pages, leaving me stunned, because I never knew how she felt when I was growing up. I was overcome with the full impact of a false idea I had created about her. It became apparent that my mother wasn't simply an angry woman lacking effective parenting skills; rather, she acted out of fear. As the second of six siblings, I experienced the effect of that fear during my upbringing. In contrast, my younger siblings were more influenced by Mom's growing calmness and self-realization, which developed after she joined the charismatic group.

My mother likely harbored considerable apprehension about presenting this speech. Besides her lack of experience addressing an audience, she grew up in a strict home environment where emotional expression was rarely acceptable, and her generation considered feelings to be very private. I imagine my mother's role in the group, her experience with Jesus, and her knowledge of the bible and prayer was why she was chosen to speak to the baptismal group.

After reviewing the notebooks and now seeing the words of the speech, it became clear to me why my mother belonged to the charismatic group–it provided a safe place to give voice to her overwhelming fears and helped her to tell this story.

When I imagine my mother in front of a baptismal group, I envision her nervousness neatly hidden under enormous strength and determination. Now I feel so proud of how she must have worked through the resistance to a place of believing she could appear in front of so many people with such a personal story.

Following, I have included the entire speech my mother wrote with heartfelt meaning for this ceremony. Presented during a mass, and part of a Life of the Spirit seminar, this was a significant talk given before people have hands laid on them and before they are baptized in the Holy Spirit.

My mother spoke of Satan several times. Today, I interpret this as the ego or dark thoughts and judgments that are simply places where we have not understood, healed, or yet brought into the light.

Speech:　Frances, my mother

Date:　　Unknown, possibly the 1980s

Next week you will be prayed over to receive the Baptism in the Holy Spirit. Jesus promised his Apostles that the Holy Spirit would come to them after He ascended into Heaven. (Read Acts 1 8 & 9 and Act 2 1-7, 14-21).

To receive the Holy Spirit, we must repent and accept Jesus as our Lord. Repentance means admitting that we have things in our lives that need changing and must be willing to change and be aware that we need God's help to change. Then we must turn away from these faults and decide not to do them anymore and ask God for forgiveness.

Once you ask the Holy Spirit to come into your heart, the Holy Spirit will teach you to repent.

With me, I could not swear, gossip, criticize or yell at the kids without right away feeling guilty and asking God's forgiveness. This week, Satan will make it difficult for you and make you think you are not worthy. I know what this means, because the past few weeks I have had quite a battle with Satan over giving this talk. This is a first for me. Every time I picked up my pencil to jot down notes on what to say, I would panic and say, 'I can't do it.'

Then I would pray and ask the Holy Spirit what to say. He would tell me, "Tell them how much you love Me and what I have done for you. Leave the rest to Me. All I need is your faith in Me. I will do the rest." As you can see, I have put my faith in Him. If you begin to get doubts and become discouraged that is Satan trying to make you think you are unworthy to receive. Never feel that you are not worthy to receive the Holy Spirit. God takes us as we are as long as we call unto Him. (Acts 2 38 & 39)

When I prayed to the Holy Spirit, the only feeling I had was my heart beat very fast. God is very gentle. Some feel nothing at all, but this does not mean that you have not received. We must ask in faith, expecting to receive because God promised this to us. Even in Ancient time, they followed God by Faith. (Heb. 11 1-8).

Jesus has so much love to give us. I have been given so many blessings. He takes care of all my family problems now. They were so overwhelming before I came to know Jesus and His love for me. I was so insecure when I was raising a family, 6 children. I always tried to do everything for them and had great fear that they would not live up to their commitments to the church and God and be living for the worldly things and be influenced by the evil in the world. When I made my first seminar, one of my girls was giving me a hard time. I can look back now and see that it was all part of her growing up. It was a very difficult time for me. My seminar leader told me that I was standing in God's way of helping her. I was told she did not belong to me, she belonged to God, and I had to give her up, turning her over completely to Jesus and let Him take care of her, and all of them. I found this difficult. It took me a long time to put my trust in God. I can remember standing in my living room, feeling completely helpless, not knowing which way to turn and I said, and I meant it, 'Jesus, I can't do anything for her. I am giving her up to you. She, they, do not belong to me, but to you.'

In a few days, things began to change. Jesus completely took over and led her from one thing to another and it has been like that ever since and this has been over 7 years. Unbelievable opportunities opened to her and since then I have been able to turn everything over to Jesus. It seems so easy now because I realize how much He loves me and will do anything I ask. I just put my trust in Him. (Read Romans 8 14-17)

Sometimes, when we are new to this closeness we have with Jesus, we find it hard to pray in a personal way. I found this prayer to Jesus very helpful. (Although this prayer was not with her typed pages, I found it among her other writings. It speaks clearly to the letting go).

(read prayer). "Oh Heavenly Father, in the name of Your Son, Jesus, I lift to you (name), this day. Lead him/her, guide him/her, show him/her the way to your Heavenly Kingdom. Let this be Your will."

Next week will be just a beginning to the gifts of the Holy Spirit. Every day will be a new awakening to the many gifts He has for you. Jesus leads you in such a gentle way that you never need to worry. He guides you through the Scriptures. That is why we should spend time in prayer and reading the Bible and meditation every day. It is good to have a special time each day and even if it is only for a short time. I find it helpful to meditate on the rosary.

I suspect I am one of the daughters who kept my mother searching for answers. Before starting my career and settling down, my mother had reasons to be in fear. Being stubborn and fiercely independent, there were times I was taking my chances, infuriating my mother and inviting her wrath. As a teenager, most of the rules I followed were my own, and I felt most free, outdoors, being with friends, dancing, skating, soaking up the sun at the beach. Many of these activities replaced schoolwork. Getting home on time was never easy and, looking back, I can see how this contributed to my mother's worrying. I didn't understand the reasons for her strict, hard and fast rules, and probably didn't want to.

The seven-year span of time my mother refers to was the time when I became aware of my need to change direction. The birth of my son was the steppingstone to settling down, knowing someone was depending on me. There was a divinely guiding force directing me through all my training choices, work experience, and relationships, continuing to move me closer to knowing my true self as I emerged from rebellion. Having a deep desire and willingness to change course, I considered every open door or opportunity. The evolving design of my life fell into place. I believe my mother was supported by Spirit the moment she knew her current situations were not working and said, in her own ego's admission of defeat, *"Jesus, I can't do anything for her. I am giving her up to you. She, they, do not belong to me, but to you."*

Chapter Thirteen

Unaware of my mother's spiritual healing process in my youth, I enjoyed noticing the gradual changes she made in letting go of the worry around me and my siblings. She came to trust us more and somehow detached herself from the details of our lives, allowing us to experience their fullness as each day came along. Mary put it eloquently when she reminded me that while living at home, we each had many opportunities to annoy our mother, which kept her focused on our lives instead of her own. When she began to focus on herself, the conflicts were over. She tenaciously followed a course that helped her grow emotionally, mentally, and spiritually.

The candid speech to the baptismal group offered us a much-needed explanation of how she transitioned from her fears and being less than what she aspired to be, to her new place of peace and trust.

Changes that became clear in our relationship with our mother were subtle and filled us with hope. One day after I had already moved out of the family home, I stopped by to say hello, and, as I entered the kitchen where I knew I would find her, she smiled and said, with no agenda, "It's nice to see you." It was beautiful to hear these long-awaited words flow so easily and sincerely from her. Experiencing this brief gesture of welcome, combined with the aroma of a familiar applesauce cake, was enough for me to respond in kind. Much later, my sister, Mary, recalled our mother voicing a similar warm greeting when she went for a visit. Alice, too, felt Mom displayed more calmness after joining the group. Mom became more interested in going out, attending retreats with friends, and having a purpose beyond being at home with the demands of parenting. My brother, Bill, noticed that she was more in tune with the Gospel and had a greater understanding of what it meant to be a follower of Jesus or to give unconditional love.

I commend my mother for staying on her spiritual path. My own challenges with her gradually disappeared as the tension eased between us. My understanding of how my spiritual journey started in the wake of hers became clearer after reading her speech.

I believe my mother beautifully and faithfully incorporated Jesus's teachings into her life. When she pursued self-awareness, or embraced the fullness of Jesus, she took to heart one of His profound, life-changing messages: "No one else is called to carry the gear of another."

In her humility, my mother kept her inner spiritual journey private from our family. She felt no need for others to understand the intricacies of her healing process. Devoid of ego, she simply radiated the light of her transformed existence.

Chapter Fourteen

There were obvious strengths possessed by the women in my mother's family, which, over time, emerged in a variety of many interesting ways. While in her younger years, my mother let fear dominate her life, she also admirably followed in her mother's footsteps, especially in standing up for necessary causes. One such cause was advocating for more education. My father was of the narrow and old-fashioned opinion that girls do not need to be in college. He said they will only get married and raise children. When it came time to discuss college in the late 1960s, my older siblings and I stood in the kitchen mortified as our father spoke these words out loud. Rarely having the chance to speak with seven other voices in the house, it was shocking to hear his strong conviction to keep us from college. Equally shocking was how my mother immediately took a strong position for my sisters and me, despite his objections. Eventually, we all attended college, enjoyed our chosen careers, found partners to marry, and raised families.

Later, in my thirties and forties, I visited my Aunt Florence whenever I had time to spend a few hours. She lived alone and part of my visit was simply to check in with her. Often, I had my mother and my Reiki table with me. Somewhere during the visit, I did healing work with both of them. Neither of them talked during a session, but expressed their gratitude for how relaxed they felt.

When my mother was not present, Florence opened up more. With her love of talking, she brought many family memories to light. I always enjoyed these revealing conversations with her because my mother and Aunt Kay so protectively held the secrets of their past. Florence became my source of buried family history. Although tea with my aunt was casual and mostly about catching up on each other's lives, there was more. I soon realized she was revealing important pieces of my mother's life, illuminating where there had been only empty spaces filled with questions.

One morning, over a good cup of tea and warm blueberry muffins dripping with butter, my Aunt Florence shared a new story with me. She shared a particular example that would further prove the strength of these women. As we sat across the table from each other in our usual chairs, cooling tea filling the stillness between us, I could see the distress in her eyes, the hesitation she had in sharing something weighing heavily on her mind and heart. She held her teacup with both hands and proceeded to release decades of repressed pain. I imagined it was daunting to live alone with her upsetting thoughts of the past overshadowing daily routines. Because we had good rapport, she felt safe to continue her story.

Florence told me about the morning she accompanied her mother to a lawyer's office to support her while she filed for a divorce from her husband, Florence's father. This was unusual at the time. As with many of our discussions about her father, I realized she was holding back some details. I respectfully kept my questions to a minimum, but with the information she did give me, I could piece together a larger picture.

While she spoke, my thoughts briefly drifted to memories of how my mother never kept alcohol in the house until we were older. Later, she constantly worried we might drink whenever we left home. Reflecting on this, my mother's unease and fears concerning alcohol in our home started to make sense. I also began to grasp how draining it must have been for my grandmother to live with my grandfather, and for my mother and aunts to grow up dealing with his temperament.

When my grandmother and aunt arrived at the lawyer's office that morning, they introduced themselves to the receptionist. My grandmother stated her purpose. After they both sat silently for six or seven hours in the waiting area with unwavering, stoic determination, the lawyer finally came out to speak to them. He had no intention of helping her with a divorce. Prior to no-fault law in 1969, divorces were not impossible, but difficult to get.

Angry and disappointed as they left the office, my grandmother saw no other choice but to leverage her ownership of their home to make her voice heard. In February 1951, she sought a different lawyer to create a will, bequeathing her house to her children upon her death, and leaving the minimum required to her husband.

It was a sad remembrance, long held in secret places within the family that she wanted me to hear. When the telling was over, she looked at me with such a sincere smile of relief. I simply said thank you, hoping it conveyed how grateful I was that she entrusted her mother's experience with me.

Aunt Florence, Kay, and my mother broke the suppressive pattern associated with alcohol in their lineage. They chose marriages that may have challenged them in many ways, yet they were less restricted and honored their rights. My mother and Aunt Kay found comfort and support in her pursuit of much needed spiritual healing through the charismatic group. Aunt Florence was also supported while pursuing her faith in her own way. All of them were models for other women in the family.

Over time, we had many more cups of tea and many more stories to share. I will always be grateful for my time with Aunt Florence.

Chapter Fifteen

As I sat deep in thought on a cool gray cement bench outside a local hospital, I found myself smiling at the swarm of tiny white butterflies fluttering around me. It was autumn 2003, and I was waiting for my husband to bring the car from the parking garage. The message the butterflies brought me that day was one of transformation, which I would not fully understand until much later. All I knew after hours in the emergency room was that my heart was beating fast for no apparent reason. Little did I know that this was the beginning of a more intense journey.

Natalia, my Reiki student in training, was with me weeks later when I had one of these episodes. She strongly and persistently recommended I meet Lydia, a woman she had worked with and felt would be helpful to me. I was already using herbal remedies and various healing techniques to manage my symptoms, which were improving, so I saw no need to look for care elsewhere. Before she moved to London, Natalia made one last attempt over lunch to encourage me to contact Lydia.

We were overlooking the canal at one of my favorite restaurants. Natalia spoke at length about the natural approach Lydia used to help speed healing. Although she did not have the language to describe this modality completely, the passion in her voice and her experience with Lydia were convincing enough. I went home and made the appointment.

Lydia used guided imagery techniques during my visits with her. They led me to remarkable self-discoveries and realizations. Amazed, I felt less anxious and had a stronger sense of stability in my heart. I could never have imagined, planned, or navigated such deep experiences alone. Lydia gently led me through doors and shadows of this lifetime and those before it. I discovered deep and long-held emotions, beliefs, habits, and behavior patterns behind the roles I play every day. Persistent in her techniques, I was drawn to the way she could help me put the fragmented pieces of my life together, providing me with valuable new perspectives. Through this process, I noticed how my heart was responding to all the ways I do things quickly. I multi-task, work through chores, talk, and even brush my teeth all too fast. Over time, my heart rate returned to normal. And I even came to view the relationship with my mother differently.

A year later, I began an intense study of the techniques Lydia called "Full Sensory Perception." It addressed everything she worked on with me, including drawing wisdom from past experiences, to understand and heal present situations. Later, I could easily include the methods into my own healing practice.

Continuing to strengthen my heart, I discovered that the most profound reward was when I sensed that my mother had begun to attend my sessions in spirit. Considering the miles separating us and the confusion of Alzheimer's, a spirit connection with her would prove a powerful way to communicate. I always knew it was Mom, as she always presented herself in ways I understood. She appeared to me with a familiar gesture, in clothes I recognized, or she stirred up old, familiar emotions.

When my mother appeared spiritually at my first healing appointment with Lydia, I felt guilt rise to the surface. I struggled with living too far from her, making it difficult to help the family with her care. My visits to Boston every few months were not enough. Unable to change my living situation, I continued to dialogue with her in spirit. The desire to work with my mother remotely was driven by the valuable life-changing realizations for me and the increasing calmness I witnessed in my mother, despite the decline in her physical health.

As our mother's illness progressed, my sister, Alice, called to let me know Mom's anxiety had returned. The call was a signal for me to connect energetically with my mother through the distant healing of Reiki and the techniques I learned from Lydia. I continued to use these methods to help her. With each encounter, I could see how she was healing. The frantic calls from Alice diminished.

Part 3

A Gift of Forgiveness

Chapter Sixteen

Although times during my sessions guided by Lydia were enlightening, it was not without discomfort for me. Sensing and feeling my mother's presence was enough to trigger the memories of old emotions of anger, fear, and negativity that I had not yet resolved. Having kept them in a dark, forgotten corner of my heart, I had judged these emotions and behaviors as hers alone. As I became aware of these feelings, which shed light on the truth, it seemed inconceivable to me that they also represented my own struggles.

With the needed support from Lydia, I could let go of the past and easily understand the reasons Mom turned to me in spirit. She beautifully reflected to me what I needed to know about myself while she, too, was healing from the experience. My willingness to look deeper at my own patterns was her opportunity.

With all our emotions so delicately revealed, Lydia greatly influenced this next phase for my mother and me. My time spent committed to stay on this course would prove to be a journey of mutual respect and forgiveness. Each encounter helped us to see the past and each other differently, allowing for previous tensions in our relationship to settle. I realized the work I was doing to release my part in our dynamics was calming her anxiety even three hundred eighty miles away.

With the strain of the past behind us, my mother began coming to me as a stronger and more peaceful spirit. The first time I felt this change in her energy, I was in my home office, struggling to concentrate on my work because of my rising anger. Earlier, I encountered someone who, through a simple gesture of not letting me teach an important technique to his friend who had sought my help, questioned the value and integrity of my work. I finally placed my work aside, pushed my chair back, and hoped that closing my eyes would help to shift these unpleasant thoughts. As soon as I took a full breath, I saw my mother in front of me in a lighter form. In a very gentle, non-judgmental, sweet, steady, and affirming voice, I heard her say, "Don't let your anger destroy you as it destroyed me."

In my experience, when someone passes, their messages may not be conveyed in the highest divine expression. My mother included the words "anger" and "destroy." Was her message valid? The real question I asked myself was, how did I feel when I heard that information? Because the words resonated and revealed an old wound, the source did not matter. Like divine messages from Jesus, Mom's message to me brought up old emotions that I needed to heal. She was still growing spiritually, as I was.

Beneath the impact of the message from my mother, I recognized the truth. In a moment of temporary irrationality, I had forgotten who I was and had allowed someone else to define me. *A Course in Miracles* would call that an error of thinking. The destructive anger I held did not serve any purpose except to hide the actual emotion of sadness. My thoughts gradually shifted to a deeper realization: this was yet another rejection of my healing practice, a practice deeply ingrained in my spirit. It reminded me of all the instances where I felt out of place because my beliefs differed from the traditional. That familiar deep inner judgmental voice came through to me to question what I was doing. Should I consider hospital work again and disregard the many years spent blending my nursing skills with natural healing?

Shortly after my mother revealed her wiser and more healed self, tranquility settled over my office once more. A deep, authoritative yet tender male voice resonated—it was that of the late Dr. Usui, the Japanese minister credited with rediscovering Reiki in the early 1900s. Back in the late 1990s, during my Reiki studies, I had the privilege of being introduced to this esteemed teacher. On that day, he delivered a significant message: *"You do not know the thousands of people you have helped."* Those words served as a potent reminder that when one person experiences healing, its ripple effect extends to everyone they encounter, much like a pebble creating gentle waves in water.

The presence and wisdom of both Dr. Usui and my mother filled me with gratitude. They reinforced the importance of my healing work, not just for myself but for others as well.

They helped me grasp that the person who triggered my anger and self-doubt played a pivotal role in exposing the pattern of vacillation between traditional and natural healing methods. Interestingly, what struck me later was the synchronicity between my mother and Dr. Usui, as they both responded to my distress simultaneously.

Chapter Seventeen

If it seems strange to communicate with people who are not right in front of you in flesh and bone, or who are deceased, I want you to know that is exactly how I felt with my first encounter. I discovered there are many advantages to this level of communication. Healing with my mother is a perfect example of the ability to experience closure and forgiveness despite the barriers of physical distance, and the fog of Alzheimer's.

Many times, when the spirits of a relative or friend come into my awareness, whether alive or deceased, they identify themselves in familiar ways, as my mother and Jesus have done. It could be a scent of pine trees and a campfire from our camping days that once connected me to my father. My grandmother might appear in her apron, awakening a warm kitchen memory, or specific clothing style that distinguished spirits from each other.

A profound example of connecting with my mother comes to mind. In the middle of one wintry night in January, I sat up in bed, coughing and feeling miserable with what I thought was bronchitis. After a few minutes, the waves of distress smoothed out, and the room fell silent.

The spirit of what I knew to be an angelic version of my mother floated into the room as a wisp of a long white gown. No part of me was uncomfortable or questioned what her presence meant. There was a readiness and peace somehow surrounding the grief I didn't need to feel right now. It was her time to go. My mother had found me to say goodbye in a language only my heart would know.

The next morning, I received a call from Alice to say that our mother was doing better than the day before and things seemed to be stable. Had I imagined the night before?

Somewhat later, I went to Urgent Care to address my cough. While waiting for the doctor, Alice called my mobile phone, now entrusted to my husband, Jack, to let me know Mom had passed peacefully. When he told me, my head dropped in exhaustion, and I whispered an acknowledgement, "I know," under my heavy sigh. Puzzled, he would have to wait for that explanation, as just then the doctor walked into the room.

What could have been a long, difficult road of grieving for me was eased by the healing prior to my mother's passing. The many hours working through the past and letting go of anger and resentment prepared me to let go of her in the physical form.

While I was agonizing over her illness, one of the strongest messages she conveyed to me was "see me here." Long before she passed, she had come to me to show me two pictures—one of herself aging with Alzheimer's, the other of her in a healed, whole way. She kept pointing to the latter, urging me to recognize her true self beyond her illness.

Another memorable moment when my mother came to me again in spirit after she had passed. During a group meditation at my drum circle in the autumn of 2010. I settled into the yurt where twenty or so members of my circle group gathered around a large buffalo hide drum to celebrate Hallowmas or All Saints' Day. It was a time to honor the departed. I closed my eyes as our beloved leader and friend, Heron, began a rhythmic pace of a strong, steady heartbeat across the drum. This rhythm gently brought me into a deep place of stillness. Shortly into the meditation, I sensed my mother kneeling at my left side.

It was unusual because my mother mostly appeared in front of me. She was pointing in a direction we were both facing across the circular tent with its many items on the canvas walls honoring all four directions. I followed her invitation towards my Uncle Bob, who was standing at the east wall. I realized my mother was acting as an intermediary, supporting me and stepping aside for my uncle. He transitioned years prior, and I had not connected to him until this moment.

My uncle had been a man of few words and true to form, his only message to me that night was "help her cross." I knew he was referring to my Aunt Florence, his wife. I went home that night confused, wondering what I should do. What in the world did he expect me to do? I had helped many souls cross over, but Aunt Florence, despite her age, was still on her feet. Later that week, he appeared to me in the early morning hours, showing an image of himself outside of my kitchen door clearly on the "other side" of the door. He stood silent, his message reminding me of what was being asked.

Over the year, I made it a point to visit Florence with the intent to just observe, be present to her and ask spirit for guidance. Months later, I heard from two of Florence's adult grandchildren. They had come to me for healing sessions in the past and were both, at different times that year, wanting to reconnect. I worked with them individually by phone (both living in different states). Each time, Florence came into the session in spirit to her grandchildren, much like my mother had. There was a beautiful exchange of the past for a new perspective in their connection to each other. This led to healing for each of them.

I soon realized that this was the way I was preparing Florence to cross. She was 97 years old and still holding onto the worry of her family... the worry my uncle clearly knew was preventing her spirit from moving on.

May 6, 2011, at 9:30 in the morning, my Aunt Florence had a stroke and was not responding. I received a call late that afternoon from my cousin Cathy. I was driving, so I pulled the car over, knowing I was about to get an update on her condition. Cathy said my aunt was still not conscious.

I invited Cathy into a short meditation to check her mother's energy. Immediately, I felt an anchor in her heart, an anchor that was holding her to this plane. I was being shown that the concern for her daughter and her daughter's family was fiercely in place. Through our meditation, Cathy was able to reassure her mother that it was okay to release her role here as a mother and grandmother and that she and the children would be fine. In holding Florence with respect, honoring her experience in this life, I gradually felt that anchor of worry drift away. Aunt Florence passed peacefully an hour later.

As I think about this experience with Florence, I recognize the gift she left our family, the gift of letting go of the worry that now seemed pointless. She and my mother were queens of worry, worrying about us, what we were doing and not doing, worrying about the neighbors and what they would think about what we were doing or not doing. It creates a vicious cycle of living in probable unhappiness and/or unsolved distractions. Seeing this pattern held so firmly until the end, I could see my own worry gene magnified. I then chose for this pattern to be revealed to me in a gentle, healing way.

Like my mother, Aunt Kay was in a nursing home for many years with Alzheimers, and she passed in 1998. In the end, my siblings and I rotated staying with her day and night. During this time, Kay developed pneumonia, so I used Reiki over her lungs to calm her breathing. When I went home one of those nights, I performed absent Reiki and had a very unusual experience. As soon as I imagined my hands were at her head, I felt an overwhelming amount of energy pour through me to her from every direction. The next day, she began to transition and eventually passed peacefully.

An extraordinary instance where a spirit appeared to me involved my first grandson. Months before he was born, I was in my car when I sensed a strong gust of wind through a closed window. A healthy, intense, older child appeared wearing a familiar plaid flannel shirt with a pocket. The shirt was my confirmation that this child was family—my son wore the same type, using the pocket as a convenient way to hide knobs, screws, and bolts he collected from places we visited.

Knowing how to get my attention, Jake, as he came to be named, let me know his parents seemed distant. He was their first child, and my son and daughter-in-law were consumed with worry about whether their baby would be healthy. However, Jake's message was clear and direct that he was fine and that he simply needed more attention from them as parents.

When I arrived at my son's house, excited to be the first to know the baby's gender, I wrote it on a piece of paper and hid it in a basket hanging in the kitchen. I then passed along Jake's message to them. Just as I thought, they were talking to him in Spirit, as if he had already arrived; however, more often they were distracted by daily life.

As a teenager now, Jake has maintained that same strong, spirited personality he showed me in the car that day. Since all three grandsons were born, I can strongly feel not only Jake, but Ben and Sam, too, coming to me at different times for ethereal visits. Often missing them, I find comfort in the sweet connection when each one lays his head on my shoulder to make his presence known.

In no order of hierarchy, Loved Ones, Ascended Masters, Spirit or Animal Guides patiently shepherd each of us on our own way until eventually, we trust our inner wise counsel.

Busyness, emotions, or grief can block our ability to sense their messages, so it is important to practice stillness every day, even for a few minutes. When I experience them and surrender any of these stressful feelings, I am better able to receive unlimited guidance. With a little practice, anyone can benefit from these amazing, sometimes life-altering, encounters.

A few of my deceased ancestors, some known to me in this lifetime and others not, still communicate directly for healing generational patterns or un-resolved details of the past. In August 2011, eight members of my family were invited to meet with a cousin who had extensively researched and com-pleted our family tree on my mother's side.

We gathered with obvious curiosity about what we would hear. My cousin, Bob, whom I did not know well until much later in life, presented a view of the genealogy software filled with names and pictures dating from 1574 England to 1879 Nova Scotia and the 1600s to 1800s in Maine and Massachusetts. Accompanied by a brief narrated story, name after name appeared on the overhead screen in his conference room. We were silently mesmerized learning about our lineage.

After Bob finished presenting his twenty-five years of research, a brief discussion followed. We expressed our gratitude for the time, passion, and determination he had invested in this family endeavor. Following his explanation of how he gathered the information, another cousin raised an intriguing question: "Why did our families not spend time with each other over the years?" This struck me as an a-ha moment! We were finally addressing the elephant in the room! Yet no one dared to voice the real answer.

Soon after I reacted to the question, I felt the room's temperature rise. I sensed the presence of a few of our ancestors in spirit form gathering around. Feeling overwhelmed, I quietly left the room to seek refuge and fresh air. However, they followed me. Their eagerness to share their stories was palpable, like children excitedly jumping around to get your attention. They seemed pleased that we were discussing them and eager to be part of our conversation. Unsure of how my family would react to their presence, I hesitated to mention it. Eventually, they consented to wait for a more suitable time, and I returned to the conference room feeling relieved.

Several ancestors, however, did not wait long to reveal themselves. Within days of the family meeting, one by one, their spirits appeared to me. They identified themselves to me in many ways by each presenting themselves as a faded image, generating an emotion, sparking a memory from the past, or giving information through words, phrases, or feelings that eventually come together to form a story. I always trust the first words, phrases, thoughts, or feelings that come to me. And I acknowledge this information without judgment and remain open to the subsequent messages.

The first ancestor was a petite, middle-aged woman in my mother's lineage from the 1800s, dressed in a long, dark-colored gown, revealed herself to me. Her presence brought a sense of sadness. Trusting this feeling, shortly after she appeared, I perceived her to be highly intuitive. Yet, because of the limited mindset of her era, she couldn't openly use her voice to share this gift with others. Forced to keep this profound secret, she never experienced the joy of embracing this inherent aspect of herself. This 1800s woman came to me because she was ready to heal her sadness. We shared a revealing moment where we acknowledged and honored each other. We decided that no matter where we are in our journey, we are safe to express our true selves. I shared with her that it took decades for me to fully embrace what I had always known. Hiding behind my degrees and qualifications long enough to grow into my gifts has enabled me gradually to stand up to the fear of what others might think. I am grateful to have had the opportunity to heal my own sadness and to help her let go of the past.

Rarely do I receive a name from a visiting spirit. However, a great, great grandfather wanted me to know his name—Ebenezer—possibly because there are two Ebenezers in our lineage. The one who came to me walked this earth sometime in the 1700s or

1800s. The first words he uttered were, "Burden of land." Immediately, I connected it with my experience that yard work and maintaining multiple gardens is an enormous task. When I asked him how he coped with the labor involved, he said he would walk the land and express appreciation for everything it gave to him.

In Ebenezer's presence, I recalled the many summer mornings I walked on my half acre property, cup of coffee in hand, planning my day in the gardens. I sat in the sun, imagining different layouts for each section and how their colorful designs would complement each neighboring plant.

I was also reminded of how my mother always created a garden or two of flowers, especially purple irises framing the right side of the front porch. Occasionally she drew one of us into tending the soil with her. More often, she arranged a bouquet to display in our familiar green ceramic vase on the dining room table.

On my first property in Upstate New York, I was excited to find a few irises scattered randomly among the flowers in each garden bed like pieces of a memory of my mother and me as we once were. Their deep purple color took me back to another time, seeing my mother tending to something other than her duties. Caring for these beautiful flowers outdoors and house plants indoors seemed to bring her continual joy. Now I understand how Ebenezer was helping me to see the gardens in a more vibrant way.

Weeks after Ebenezer appeared, a meek and reserved woman, possibly in her thirties or forties, made her strong presence felt with a powerful message in the briefest of moments. Meek is not a word I typically used, but it seemed important to focus on that word in her message. She came to stress, "We, as women, have power even in our meekness. It is how we survived." I understood the strength she had found. If we consider the social climate of her time, it was dangerous to speak out. I admired this strength she had and the intuitive ability to know when it was safe to express herself. Her senses were most likely heightened within her chosen silence.

This encounter with my ancestor beautifully highlighted the strength of meekness today, especially in accepting the world as it is. Stepping back allows me to observe and gives me time to look deeper at my own reactions to people and events.

Jesus continues to call me back to myself, to release my fears, and to bring my thoughts back to a neutral place of peace. Without my own personal agenda and emotions blocking the way, I can only send love and shine my light towards any situation.

After moving to another town in 2009, Ebenezer came into my awareness a few more times during my early morning walks in the following years. One day when I stopped to rest on a bench, I saw a faded image of a tall figure appear in front of me, leaning casually against an old oak tree that matched his massive presence. Ebenezer was quiet, appearing to be simply an observer while my paternal grandfather, we called Pa, took a seat on my right side to comfort me. Gently patting my knee, in a supporting way, he softly uttered, *"It will be alright."* This confused me, as nothing distressful was happening in my life, yet I allowed this moment to unfold.

Shortly after, I was compelled to sit on the grass, feeling bewildered as I sensed my close friend, Jason, sitting opposite me. Looking at him triggered a tumultuous surge of emotions, which was immediately succeeded by an overpowering, intense fear of what it would mean to lose him. I was left questioning the significance of this experience. It was 9:30 a.m.

Once back home, I started a long day filled with waiting, weighed down by the heaviness of that meditation. Questions flooded my mind. Was this about his contract ending? We had discussed it from time to time, and I thought I was ready for when he would eventually leave New York. Why would Spirit stir up such intense feelings of losing him? Little did I know, the two grandfathers had a specific purpose for visiting me that day. They wanted to make me realize the importance of my relationship with Jason and to ensure I didn't take it for granted. After all, we had been friends for twelve years; the loss would undoubtedly be immense if something happened to him. That day, I truly felt the potential depth of that loss.

Then, around 2:30 p.m. I received an alarming text from Jason, calmly stating that he had had a heart attack that morning at 6:00 a.m. However, after a procedure, he felt better and assured me his family was on their way and I did not have to rush to the hospital. After nervously pacing, texting, and exchanging logistic information from my patio, I realized I needed to hear his voice. I knew if I did, I would have a better sense of how worried I needed to be. Humoring me, he called. It was encouraging to hear his familiar energetic southern accent clearly over the phone. Although trusting my own abilities, I wanted Jason's intuitive perception about my spiritual encounter that morning. I would have to wait.

Ebenezer appeared to me again, this time to highlight a deeply entrenched family pattern. He jokingly said, "We are a stiff bunch." I could not help but smile at the potent English influence that threads its way through our lineage. Without warning, that thought turned into a feeling of stiffness in my body, drawing my focus to the many suppressed thoughts and memories associated with that stoic demeanor. After a few minutes, these emotions released their hold on me. Relieved of the intensity of this experience, I noticed Ebenezer was unmoved, simply a witness to my new realization, as Jesus often is. It was time for me to let my guards down and allow excitement and joy to flow through. I imagined my connectedness to my mother would have offered her the same awareness of this family pattern in the lineage.

Although the ancestors were not focused on our interpersonal family drama, I was curious and took this opportunity to ask Ebenezer what I needed to know about my mother's experience in her home growing up. Without hesitation, he told me, "It was difficult for her to live in the house. She was, however, the light within the family, but her true soul mission was with Aunt Kay, as their work together was important to the whole." His counsel surprised me because it reflected a notebook entry where Jesus referred to my mother and Aunt Kay as prayer partners. He also asked that we, as a family, look beyond the details of the family story to concentrate on the importance of forgiveness.

Chapter Eighteen

Perhaps Mom hoped that the discovery of her notebooks by any of her children would deepen our faith. No matter what we do with our lives or what faith we follow, she gently continues to send her wisdom and make her loving presence known through the veils, as my other ancestors have done. She teaches us there is very little separating our souls and there is always another way to look at things. Whether or not my family has joined her in the faith she knew, I believe she is not disappointed.

Faith in my healing abilities grows stronger every day. Although encouragement from others is welcome, this is my own inward journey towards knowing and accepting who I am. Unaware of the details of my mother's healing process at the time, I was strongly influenced by how it changed her. My mother relied on her connection to the charismatic group and the caring messages from Jesus as counsel and support to become the strong woman I knew her to be. I am honored my mother turned to me, and that I could eventually turn to her in healing and forgiveness. My relationship with Jesus and my mother has opened a place in my heart to accept Him as a blessed multi-dimensional Ascended Master and, through His words and hers, I have found my own expression.

As time goes by, I now more fully recognize the illusion of barriers and the thin veils that separate our souls from each other. Encounters with my mother, her lineage, and Jesus, have helped me to understand the depths of "Oneness." This wonderful heart opening inter-connectedness is the grandest opportunity for each of us to heal. Those around us who once reflected our pain and suffering will now reflect our more divine essence as we grow in consciousness.

While writing *Turn to Me,* I realized the importance of surrendering problems and letting go of my egotistical thoughts long enough to allow miracles to enter the realm of my reality. Relationships and experiences in life have become valuable gifts, offering a variety of gateways to my spirit's agenda.

Now I am turning to you, extending my invitation to recognize your own inner guide and to consider every interaction as an opportunity to heal the past and embrace the Oneness with all that you see before you and within you.

Conclusion

My mother was the wave that gently, sometimes wildly, placed me on the shore of a new truth. I emerged from a place of judging her for praying her way through my childhood at the expense of communicating directly to me. Eventually, inner exploration and the process of writing this book helped me to unravel my own buried anger and regrets. Her faith and practice of turning to Jesus have allowed me to feel the deepest sense of gratitude for how this story continues.

The first week in the new year of 2007, temperatures in Boston were dropping quickly, but the sun shone brightly. Again, it was also the time my mother passed away quietly and peacefully, entering a new dimensional world that allowed us to communicate at levels beyond my imagination.

By that spring, when the land gracefully accepted its invitation to awaken from slumber, I noticed irises emerging in all four of my gardens. For the first time in seven years, they arrived in tall masses to greet the welcoming warmer air, slowly unfurling their beauty. Amazed, I looked out over the yard towards their large clusters of purple blossoms, not only in the defined gardens but also spilling generously down the back hill. I remained silent, absorbing their gifts and their spiritual reflection of, not only strength, courage, and wisdom, but that of the relationship with my mother now in full bloom. Within this enchanting, magical moment, I sensed the ethereal presence of her letting me know she was with us and more joyous than ever.

Turn in True Acceptance of Your Own Light,
Janice

The Purple Iris

Each spring I eagerly wait for the first
brilliant dark purple Bearded Iris to
emerge from its winter covering to
absorb the first glimpse of warm sunlight.

Throughout the years, I have come to
understand the deep spiritual significance
of the Purple Iris.

It holds various symbolic meanings for both
my mother and me, but above all, it acts as a
conduit between the celestial realm and our
earthly existence.

The creation of this book was possible because of you who came to me with patience, friendship, various expertise, talents, and wise counsel. I especially extend my heartfelt appreciation to each of you for encouraging me in this endeavor. You demonstrated your ability to keep your eyes on the broader picture, gave me advice to clarify important content, and asked me pointed questions to bring forth and enrich my story. Know that your special contribution will always be an inherent part of my book's message.

I am sincerely grateful to my family for the many conversations we had recalling the details of our history, but most of all, for the sheer enjoyment of reliving past moments with each of you.

As always, much love to my son, Jason, for his strength and fortitude over the last few years. He was my first reason to change the direction of my life and will always be one of my greatest teachers.

The story began with the purpose of sharing my mother's notebooks with my family. Eventually, I realized our important dual journey could appeal to a wider audience. I am grateful to my mother for taking meticulous notes, thanks to her church group, and saving the notebooks for the benefit of generations to come.

MY WARMEST GRATITUDE TO:

Wayne Chatterton
Jeanne Crane
Seema Khaneja
Jack McNamara
Amy Miller
Bill Proulx
Sue Whan
Francisca de Zwager

About the Author

Janice McNamara, a nurse for 38 years and the founder of Next Step Holistic, is a Reiki Master Teacher and Associate Polarity Practitioner, using her intuitive abilities for healing. With a blend of humor, she bridges the gap between traditional and integrated practices, offering individual and holistic guidance. Janice helps adults and children uncover underlying thoughts and beliefs to reconnect with their authentic selves. Her wisdom empowers them to nurture intuition, expand awareness, and infuse joy into every aspect of life. In return, they continually remind her of the Divine Light within.

For information about Janice and her services, go to www.nextstepholistic.com/